FUSION WITH GOD

THE PATH TO IMMORTALITY

MICHAEL VINCENT

First Edition, 2026

ISBN: 978-1-971762-99-9

CONTENTS

A NOTE ON LANGUAGE

Throughout this book, God is referred to as "Father" and with masculine pronouns ("he," "him," "his"). This requires explanation.

First, understand what God is not:

> *God is neither manlike nor machinelike. The First Father is universal spirit, eternal truth, infinite reality, and father personality.*[1]

God transcends gender entirely. He is spirit, not biological. The masculine terminology is about relationship, not gender.

So why "Father"?

> *On a planet of sex creatures, in a world where the impulses of parental emotion are inherent in the hearts of its intelligent beings, the term Father becomes a very expressive and appropriate name for the eternal God.*[2]

We are gendered beings who understand love through parental relationships. The term "Father" communicates intimate, personal care in ways impersonal terms cannot. It speaks to a longing within us.

Those who know God through the revelations of the bestowals of the Paradise Sons, eventually yield to the sentimental appeal of the touching relationship of the creature-Creator association and refer to God as 'our Father.'[3]

Language born from relationship, not theology. It emerges naturally when creatures truly encounter their Creator.

He is best known, most universally acknowledged, on your planet by the name God. The name he is given is of little importance; the significant thing is that you should know him and aspire to be like him.[4]

The point is not the word but the reality behind it. And what is that reality?

As a father, a real father, a true father, loves his children, so the Universal Father loves and forever seeks the welfare of his created sons and daughters. But the love of God is an intelligent and farseeing parental affection.

The Father's love follows us now and throughout the endless circle of the eternal ages.[5]

Why use "Father"? To convey the nature of divine love: personal, protective, intelligent, eternal, and utterly devoted to your welfare.

When you read "Father" in these pages, hear it as an invitation to intimacy rather than a biological assertion. God is your Father in the deepest, truest, most perfect sense—and that relationship transcends all categories of gender.

One more note on terminology. Throughout this book, you will encounter variations on the term "Thought Adjuster" in quoted passages. This is one of several names given to the indwelling spirit, and it deserves a brief explanation.

The name describes what this presence does — it adjusts your thinking. Not by force, not by overriding your will, but by gently elevating your thoughts toward higher meanings and spiritual values. It works with your thinking, refining it, spiritualizing it, adjusting it upward.

The name actually changes as the relationship deepens. In youth, when the spirit is first shaping a newly forming mind, it is called a Thought Changer. In the middle years, as it works alongside your maturing will, it becomes a Thought Adjuster. And in later life, when the partnership has grown strong and the spirit's influence becomes more directive, it is called a Thought Controller. These names reflect not different beings but different phases of one growing relationship —the same divine presence, doing deeper work as you become capable of receiving it.

Other names appear as well: divine monitor, divine gift, indwelling spirit, Father fragment. Each name illuminates a different facet of the same extraordinary reality. In this book, I generally use more accessible terms like "indwelling spirit" or "divine spirit."

INTRODUCTION

What if the most important relationship in your life, the one that determines your eternal destiny, is one you barely know exists?

What if, right now, dwelling within the most intimate chambers of your mind, there is a presence—not an idea, not a feeling, not your conscience or intuition, but an actual fragment of the Divine, living and working within you, loving you with a patience and devotion that would stagger you if you could perceive even a fraction of it?

And what if this presence has been with you since childhood, waiting, hoping, working tirelessly toward a single magnificent goal: to become one with you forever?

You may have heard variations of this idea before. But what follows is not vague mysticism. It is specific, detailed, and testable in your own experience.

Here is its central claim: within you dwells a fragment of God. This is the most profound reality of human existence, a reality most people live and die without fully grasping.

The indwelling spirit is the actuality of the Father's love incarnate in the souls of men.[1]

And this divine presence is not merely visiting. It is not temporarily assigned. Its mission chiefly concerns your future eternal life, not your present mortal existence, yet it works tirelessly within your present experience to prepare you for that future.

This spirit of infinity will ultimately fuse with you, will unite so completely with your personhood that you and it become an eternal, inseparable unity, a new order of being that transcends both humanity and divinity as they currently exist separately. But this doesn't happen all at once. Your soul is being built, choice by choice, insight by insight, from the raw material of your mortal experience and the divine pattern the spirit carries. Everything of genuine worth that happens in your life is being translated into what will survive your death. The spirit is not merely watching you live. It is harvesting your temporal life for an eternal one.

This fusion is your destiny. It is what you were made for. It is the purpose behind your existence and the goal toward which all your spiritual striving tends.

> *Eternal fusion with the indwelling spirit is the factual experience of eternal union with God as a universe associate of Deity.*[2]

And when it happens, when that moment of fusion finally arrives, you will be so transformed that you will look back on your mortal life as a caterpillar might look back on its crawling days. You will become, in the truest sense, immortal—not merely surviving death, but transcending it so completely that death becomes impossible, unthinkable, a condition that simply no longer applies to your being.

This book is about that fusion. About the relationship that makes it possible. About what happens when it occurs. And about how you can consciously cooperate with this divine process even now, to the tremendous benefit of both your present existence and your eternal future.

This comes from a source that describes the indwelling spirit, the soul, and the fusion that awaits in such extraordinary detail that the mystery becomes a map. What it reveals may astonish you.

What follows is not a system of philosophic belief to be reasoned out, nor a fantastic mystic experience of indescribable ecstasy. It is something far more real—the experiencing of divinity in the consciousness of a moral being, true experience with eternal realities in time, the realization of spiritual satisfactions while yet in the flesh.

> *Every God-knowing mortal who has espoused the career of doing the Father's will has already embarked upon the long, long Paradise trail of divinity pursuit and perfection attainment.*[3]

1

———

THE GIFT

CLOSE YOUR EYES FOR A MOMENT. NOT TO MEDITATE, NOT TO PRAY, just to consider: What is happening in your mind right now?

Thoughts arise, seemingly from nowhere. Impulses surface, some noble, some base. Memories flood back unbidden. Plans form and dissolve. Your mind is a constant churning of activity, much of it autonomous, happening without your conscious direction.

But there is something else, something you may have never noticed. It doesn't think your thoughts. It observes them, responds to them, and constantly works with them in ways too subtle for normal consciousness to detect.

> *The infinity of the perfection of God is such that it eternally constitutes him mystery. And the greatest of all the unfathomable mysteries of God is the phenomenon of the divine indwelling of mortal minds. The manner in which the Universal Father sojourns with the creatures of time is the most profound of all universe mysteries; the divine presence in the mind of man is the mystery of mysteries.[1]*

1

Within the depths of your mind, in the highest and most refined levels of your consciousness, dwells a fragment of God—a living, conscious piece of the Universal Father himself.

The love this presence bears for you is beyond human comprehension. It is beyond parental love, though it is divinely Fatherlike in its devotion.

> *The love of the Sons in their ministry to the races is superb, but the devotion of an Adjuster to the individual is touchingly sublime, divinely Fatherlike. The Paradise Father has apparently reserved this form of personal contact with his individual creatures as an exclusive Creator prerogative. And there is nothing in all the universe of universes exactly comparable to the marvelous ministry of these impersonal entities that so fascinatingly indwell the children of the evolutionary planets.*[2]

This fragment of infinity has volunteered to share your life, to experience reality through your eyes, to grow with you toward a destiny neither of you could achieve alone.

This indwelling spirit is neither your soul nor your conscience, though it influences both. It is not you, but it is more intimately connected to you than any other being in the universe possibly could be. It is a gift, the Father's direct, divine, perfect gift to you, placed within you freely, without condition, without your asking, before you even knew such a thing was possible.

This divine presence arrived in your youth when you made your first true moral decision. *You wanted to be good.* That choice, however small it seemed, was momentous. It signaled that a living personality had emerged, a will capable of choosing, a being who could begin to *know* God and desire to *be like* God.

And the moment that capacity awakened, the Father responded. He sent his gift. And it has been with you ever since.

The indwelling spirit is the veritable promise of man's eternal career imprisoned within the mortal mind.[3]

And yet most people spend their lives searching externally for what already dwells internally.

What a mistake to dream of God far off in the skies when the spirit of the Universal Father lives within your own mind![4]

So let's be precise about what this indwelling spirit actually is, because the reality is far more staggering than any vague notion of "divine presence" or "inner light" suggests.

This is an actual fragment of God. Not a creation of God, not made by God to represent him, but actual deity—a portion of the Universal Father himself, who voluntarily fragments his infinite being to dwell in the finite mind of a mortal creature.

Think about that. The Infinite has given of itself to be present in you. The Source of all reality, the First Cause, the Creator of universes, has sent a living piece of himself to reside within you. Why would God do such a thing?

The deepest reason is that the Father is personal, and personal beings desire communion with other persons. The Infinite chose not to remain alone—he created a universe not only of things but of persons, beings capable of knowing him and being known by him.

Our Father is not in hiding; he is not in arbitrary seclusion. He has mobilized the resources of divine wisdom in a never-ending effort to reveal himself to the children of his universal domains. There is an infinite grandeur and an inexpressible generosity connected with the majesty of his love which causes him to yearn for the association of every created being who can comprehend, love, or approach him.[5]

You exist because God desired someone to share reality with. Communion with you is the very thing his heart desires.

Every person who has ever lived—every person who will ever live—is known to him. Not as a name on a list, but as a child in his arms. The indwelling spirit individualizes the love of God to each human soul. The spirit within you carries a love shaped specifically for you—a love that crossed an unimaginable distance to find you.

The gap between infinity and finitude is vast—not just physical distance, though that alone is staggering, but a gulf of spiritual reality that separates the finite creature from the Paradise presence of God. And yet God has already bridged it. He has sent of himself, his own spirit, to live within you and to toil with you as you pursue your eternal universe career. He did not wait for you to find your way across. He came to you.

And the means by which he accomplishes this partnership is extraordinary. This fragment is prepersonal but purposeful. It is not yet a person in the full sense. It will only achieve full personality status when and if it fuses with you. Until then, it exists in a state of divine intention, absolutely focused on your wellbeing and development.

It is pure spirit, not material in any sense. It cannot be detected by any physical instrument. It exists on a level of reality so refined that even your soul, which is partially spiritual, cannot fully perceive it.

It is absolutely faithful. It will never leave you, never abandon you, never betray you, never tire of working with you. Its entire existence is dedicated to one purpose: helping you achieve eternal survival and eventual fusion.

And it is infinite in potential. Though it dwells in the tiniest compass of your mind, it contains within itself the full character and pattern of the Infinite. It is God in miniature, infinity focused to a point, eternity concentrated in a moment.

> *These divine gifts are undiluted and unmixed divinity, unqualified and unattenuated parts of Deity; they are of God, and as far as we are able to discern, they are God.*[9]

Because God is infinite, you are being invited into a partnership with no ceiling, no limit, no end.

The divine presence that shares your inner life observes every thought, experiences every feeling, witnesses every choice. To help you, to guide you, to love you with a love so pure and so patient that it defies mortal comprehension.

> *The divine spirit's mission is to represent, to be, the Universal Father to the mortal creatures of time and space.*[10]

It stayed with you through your darkest hours. It held vigil when you felt most alone. It was there when you failed and when you succeeded, when you prayed and when you cursed, when you reached toward it and when you forgot it existed.

> *The endowment of imperfect beings with freedom entails inevitable tragedy, and it is the nature of the perfect ancestral Deity to univer-*

It has never once looked away. It has never once stopped working for your good. And it has never once stopped hoping you would turn around and notice what has been loving you all along.

The spirit does not control you. It does not override your will, does not control your choices, does not manipulate you into compliance. To do so would defeat the purpose of you developing a *voluntary* relationship of love and trust between you and God. Instead, it works in far subtler ways.

It spiritualizes your thinking. When you entertain a noble thought, when you aspire to truth or beauty or goodness, when you wrestle with deep questions about meaning and purpose, the indwelling spirit is *there*, enhancing that thought, elevating it, helping it reach higher levels of insight than you could achieve alone.

Over time, this constant uplifting influence changes the structure of your mind. You become capable of thoughts you couldn't think before. Concepts that once seemed impossibly abstract become clear. Truths you couldn't grasp suddenly make sense. This is not education in the ordinary sense; it is *transformation*. Your mind is being spiritualized, made capable of perceiving realities it was blind to before.

It is your thoughts, not your feelings, that lead you Godward.[12]

The pathway to divine contact runs through the mind. Many expect spiritual experience to begin with feelings—a warm glow, a surge of peace. But the sequence is usually reversed.

The divine spirit makes contact with mortal man, not by feelings or emotions, but in the realm of the highest and most spiritualized thinking.[13]

Feelings often follow, but thinking opens the door. And what comes through that door is preserved forever. The indwelling spirit remembers everything. Your mortal memory is faulty, incomplete, subject to distortion and decay. But the divine fragment remembers *everything*, every moment of spiritual significance, every decision of moral importance, every experience of authentic value. Nothing is lost.

When you die, your memory will dissolve with your physical brain. But everything worth keeping, everything that defines who you really are, will be preserved in the indwelling spirit's memory. And when you awaken to eternal life, that memory will be restored to you. You will remember everything worthwhile from your earthly life.

The Divine is preserving the substance of your life. The wisdom you gained. The love you gave. The meaning you discovered. All of it is held in eternal safekeeping.

> *The indwelling spirit never fails; nothing worth surviving is ever lost; every meaningful value in every will creature is certain of survival.* [14]

Let that sink in. Nothing of genuine value is ever lost. Not one act of love, not one moment of real courage, not one hard-won insight. All of it is preserved.

We are ennobled and energized when we learn that the higher urges of the soul emanate from the spiritual forces that indwell the mind. It lifts us out of and beyond ourselves when we realize that there lives within us something which is eternal and divine.

And it does more than inspire us—it links us to infinity. Your inner spirit is never separated from its source, never cut off from the infinite circuits of deity. Through it, the Father knows you intimately. Through it, your sincere worship reaches directly to the heart of God.

You have direct access to the Creator of all things, and you have it because a fragment of that Creator lives in you.

It is the cosmic window through which the finite creature may faith-glimpse the certainties and divinities of limitless Deity, the Universal Father.[15]

2

THE GIVER

WHO SENDS THIS GIFT? THE NATURE OF THE INDWELLING SPIRIT CANNOT be grasped apart from the nature of the One who sends it.

Who is this God who fragments himself to dwell in mortal minds? What kind of being voluntarily divides infinity to share existence with finite creatures?

At the center of all things, at the geographic and spiritual center of all reality, dwells the Universal Father. There is an actual place, an eternal isle called Paradise, and the Father is personally present there. From this center, all reality radiates outward. From this source, all existence flows.

But the Father is not confined to Paradise. That is merely his personal dwelling, his home address in eternity. His presence extends throughout all creation, his consciousness encompasses all that exists, his love reaches to the outermost edges of reality and beyond, into regions not yet created.

God is not hiding from any of his creatures. He is unapproachable to so many orders of beings only because he "dwells in a light which no material creature can approach." The immensity and grandeur of the divine personality is beyond the grasp of the unperfected mind of evolutionary mortals.[1]

The universe was not an accident. It was not a cosmic experiment or a random occurrence. It was created with purpose.

The myriads of planetary systems were all made to be eventually inhabited by many different types of intelligent creatures, beings who could know God, receive the divine affection, and love him in return.[2]

The Father wanted children. He wanted beings who could genuinely choose to love him back.

Yet the astonishing truth is that the Infinite One actively seeks relationship with finite creatures. Because love, by its nature, desires communion. As a human father naturally longs for connection with his children, how much more does the God of infinite love desire communion with his universe creatures?

First and last—eternally—the infinite God is a Father.[3]

You have been taught that God loves you. But the words have become worn smooth with repetition, their meaning dulled by familiarity. Let's restore their edge.

God manifests himself to the universes as love. In all his personal relations with the creature personalities of the universes, he is always and consistently a loving Father in the highest sense of the term. He is eternally motivated by the perfect idealism of divine love, and that tender nature finds its strongest expression and greatest satisfaction in loving and being loved.

You are not one of billions, interchangeable and expendable. You are irreplaceable. There has never been another you, and there never will be. The Father's love does not address humanity in general; it addresses you specifically, uniquely, as the particular person you are.

And this love requires nothing from you to earn it.

> *God is inherently kind, naturally compassionate, and everlastingly merciful. Never is it necessary that any influence be brought to bear upon the Father to call forth his loving-kindness. The creature's need is wholly sufficient to ensure the full flow of the Father's tender mercies and his saving grace.*[4]

You do not need to earn God's attention. You do not need intermediaries to plead your case. The Father himself loves you—not because you are good, but because he is good.

> *It is wrong to think of God as being coaxed into loving his children because of the sacrifices of his Sons or the intercession of his subordinate creatures, 'for the Father himself loves you.' It is in response to this paternal affection that God sends the marvelous Adjusters to indwell the minds of men.*[5]

The indwelling spirit is not a reward for good behavior. It is an act of love — given freely, before you asked, before you even knew it was possible.

This does not mean the Father shields you from difficulty or prevents you from suffering consequences. Divine love is intelligent, farseeing, and concerned with your eternal welfare rather than your momentary comfort. A good human father does not give his child everything the child wants. He gives what the child needs, what serves the child's development, what prepares the child for mature existence. Divine love operates similarly but with infinite wisdom to know what is truly needed and infinite patience to wait for maturation.

> *Though the Father neither makes mistakes, harbors regrets, nor experiences sorrows, he is a being with a father's affection, and his heart is undoubtedly grieved when his children fail to attain the spiritual levels they are capable of reaching.*[6]

He cares. He is invested. Your success matters to him. And the proof of that investment is the gift itself.

> *After all, the greatest evidence of the goodness of God and the supreme reason for loving him is the indwelling gift of the Father, who so patiently awaits the hour when you both shall be eternally made one.[7]*

But is such a thing even possible? How can a creature of time know the God of eternity? How can a material being comprehend pure spirit? How can the limited touch the unlimited? The Father solves the problem himself. He lovingly and willingly attenuates his own infinity, modifying his incomprehensible magnitude so that he can draw nearer to the finite minds of his creature children.

> *If the finite mind of man is unable to comprehend how so great and so majestic a God as the Universal Father can descend from his eternal abode in infinite perfection to fraternize with the individual human creature, then such a finite intellect must rest assurance of divine fellowship upon this truth: an actual fragment of the living God resides within the intellect of every normal-minded and morally conscious mortal.[8]*

You do not have to go farther than your own inner experience to find God and attempt communion with him. And you are not the only one. Across every inhabited world in the cosmos, the same gift is given.

> *In endless profusion the gifts of the great God himself descend from the heights of glory to grace and indwell the humble minds of those mortals who possess the capacity for God-consciousness.[9]*

It is not a distant deity dispatching a representative. It is the Father himself taking up residence in your consciousness. When you commune with the divine presence, you are communing with God— not with an angel, not with an intermediary, but with the actual God of all creation.

And the Father is not merely a force, not merely a principle, not merely the ground of being. He is all of these — power, energy, pattern, presence — but he is more. He is personal. He exercises a sovereign will, pursues the realization of an eternal purpose, and manifests a Father's love and affection for his universe children. He is a person, and persons can be known.

> *Man does not achieve union with God as a drop of water might find unity with the ocean. Man attains divine union by progressive reciprocal spiritual communion, by personality intercourse with the personal God.*[10]

This means you are not absorbed into God. You are not dissolved or erased. You remain you while growing ever closer to the One who made you. And that closeness has a direction. It is leading somewhere.

> *Though you cannot find God by searching, if you will submit to the leading of the indwelling spirit, you will be unerringly guided, step by step, life by life, through universe upon universe, and age by age, until you finally stand in the presence of the Paradise personality of the Universal Father.*[11]

The spirit is your guide to this knowing. It is not merely preparing you for some distant future encounter. It is introducing you to God now, progressively, as you become capable of receiving him. Every genuine moment of worship, every true perception of divine presence, and every real experience of communion are encounters with God himself, through the spirit that dwells within you.

> *However mortals may differ in their intellectual, social, economic, and even moral opportunities, forget not that their spiritual endowment is uniform and unique. They all enjoy the same divine presence of the gift from the Father, and they are all equally privileged to seek intimate personal communion with this indwelling spirit of divine origin.*[12]

The wealthy and the poor, the educated and the simple, the famous and the obscure—all receive the same gift. All are equally loved. All have the same access to the Divine.

What does the Infinite want from you? Your development, because the person you could become is worth becoming. Your love, because love is the purest joy and the highest reality, and he wants you to experience it fully. Your partnership, because working together creates bonds that working apart cannot.

But what can you possibly give to a being who already possesses everything? There is only one thing—your will.

> *In God, man lives, moves, and has his being; there is nothing which man can give to God except this choosing to abide by the Father's will, and such decisions, effected by the intelligent will creatures of the universes, constitute the reality of that true worship which is so satisfying to the love-dominated nature of the Creator Father.* [13]

Your choice, freely given, is the one thing in all the universe that the Infinite cannot produce on his own. He must wait for you to give it. This is not a limitation; it is the nature of love. Love cannot be compelled. It can only be offered and received.

> *God is not only the determiner of destiny; he is man's eternal destination. All nonreligious human activities seek to bend the universe to the distorting service of self; the truly religious individual seeks to identify the self with the universe and then to dedicate the activities of this unified self to the service of the universe family of fellow beings, human and superhuman.* [14]

The Father invites you into partnership with the universe itself, not as servant to master, but as child to parent, and eventually as friend to friend. The indwelling spirit is the beginning of this partnership, the training ground where you learn to work with deity before you can work alongside it.

If such a human mind is sincerely and spiritually motivated, if such a human soul desires to know God and become like him, honestly wants to do the Father's will, there exists no negative influence of mortal deprivation nor positive power of possible interference which can prevent such a divinely motivated soul from securely ascending to the portals of Paradise.[15]

Nothing can stop you. Not your past, not your limitations, not your failures—nothing can prevent a willing soul from reaching God. And the reason nothing can stop you is the very presence that dwells within you now. When the spirit arrived, the Father arrived. When it works within your mind, the Father works. When you finally fuse with this divine fragment, you fuse with God.

And yet even now, even with so much at stake, the Father does not force the issue.

The Universal Father never imposes any form of arbitrary recognition, formal worship, or slavish service upon the intelligent will creatures of the universes. The evolutionary inhabitants of the worlds of time and space must of themselves—in their own hearts—recognize, love, and voluntarily worship him.[16]

The Father could compel your worship. But compelled love is not real love, and compelled worship is not true worship. So the Father waits. He sends his fragment to dwell within you, to court you from the inside, to reveal himself gradually as you become capable of receiving the revelation.

The Father is not in spiritual hiding, but so many of his creatures have hidden themselves away in the mists of their own willful decisions.[17]

He has already come to you. He dwells within you now. The question is not whether God is present but whether you will turn toward that presence, acknowledge it, cooperate with it, and eventually unite with it forever.

3

THE PARTNERSHIP

The indwelling spirit cannot work alone. Despite its divine nature, despite its infinite potential, it is entirely dependent on *your* cooperation.

Why? Because God has chosen to respect your will absolutely. He will not save you against your wishes. He will not force transformation upon you. No being, force, or agency in all the wide universe of universes can interfere to any degree with the absolute sovereignty of your free will as it operates regarding your eternal destiny. God himself has decreed this sovereignty, and that decree is absolute.

So this spark of divinity waits. It offers. It suggests. It illuminates. But it cannot act unless you choose to act. It cannot grow unless you choose to grow. The entire process of spiritual evolution depends on your willing cooperation.

> *While you are in nature evolving inward and upward from man to God, the divine spirit is in nature evolving outward and downward from God to man.*[1]

This is the partnership at the heart of reality: the infinite working with the finite, the perfect patiently perfecting the imperfect, God and

17

human joining hands to create someone that could not exist without both of them—an eternal, fused being who will forever bear the marks of both origins.

> *In the final analysis, whatever the divine spirit has succeeded in doing for you, the records will show that the transformation has been accomplished with your cooperative consent; you will have been a willing partner in the attainment of every step of the tremendous transformation of the ascension career.*[2]

The records of eternity will not show that things were done to you. They will show that things were done with you. Every transformation, every step forward, every advance—you were there, consenting, participating, partnering. It's a collaboration.

And like any collaboration, it requires something from you. It requires faith. Not blind faith, not faith despite evidence, but faith that reaches beyond what can be proven. A sublime trust in the goodness of the universe, in the reality of spiritual values, in that meaning and purpose are not illusions but the deepest truths of existence.

Your spirit cannot work effectively with a mind that believes the universe is meaningless, that consciousness is accidental, that moral values are mere evolutionary adaptations. It needs the foundation of faith to build upon.

But understand the difference between faith and mere belief.

> *Belief is always limiting and binding; faith is expanding and releasing. Belief fixates, faith liberates.*[3]

And faith, unlike belief, cannot be inherited or borrowed. Belief may become group property; living faith must be personal. You can share beliefs with others, but faith you must discover and live for yourself.

> *Faith is a living attribute of genuine personal religious experience. Living faith does not foster bigotry, persecution, or intolerance.*[4]

Faith is the foundation. But the partnership also requires choice. Every day brings countless decisions, most of them small, some of them significant. The indwelling spirit is involved in all of them, subtly presenting the higher alternative, the more loving response, the more truthful path. But you must *choose* it.

> *Man, in his spiritual domain, does have a free will. Mortal man is neither a helpless slave of the inflexible sovereignty of an all-powerful God nor the victim of the hopeless fatality of a mechanistic cosmic determinism. Man is most truly the architect of his own eternal destiny.*[5]

Every choice shapes you. Every decision makes you more or less the person you are capable of becoming. The indwelling spirit can show you the way, but you must walk it.

And there is a third requirement. The partnership requires communion. When you pray, not just petitionary prayer, but genuine communion, you open channels of communication that allow the spirit to work more effectively.

Think of it as two people trying to move a heavy object together. They can do it, but it's much easier if they can communicate, coordinate, and synchronize their efforts. Your conscious cooperation in worship and prayer provides that synchronization.

And when you pray, pray for values, not things; for growth, not for gratification.

> *Prayer is not a technique of escape from conflict but rather a stimulus to growth in the very face of conflict.*[6]

And prayer changes things—not by changing God, but by changing the one who prays. Sincere prayer in faith and confident expectation transforms the person offering it. The sincere approach to the divine presence opens channels that transform the soul.

Real praying does attain reality. Even when the air currents are ascending, no bird can soar except by outstretched wings.[7]

Faith, choice, communion—these are how you spread your wings. And what they sustain is the most important relationship of your existence. If nurtured and honored, it will last forever. The being you will become billions of years from now will still carry within it the fruits of this cooperation, still be shaped by this intimacy.

You are not alone. You have never been alone. From the moment that divine spirit arrived, you have been walking hand in hand with God, whether you knew it or not.

The divine fragments are playing the sacred and superb game of the ages; they are engaged in one of the supreme adventures of time in space. And how happy they are when your cooperation permits them to lend assistance in your short struggles of time as they continue to prosecute their larger tasks of eternity.[8]

Your divine monitor experiences joy when you cooperate. Your partnership matters to the spirit, not just to you. When you turn inward, when you reach toward God, when you align your will with divine purposes, the spirit rejoices. This is not a one-sided relationship. Both partners are invested. Both partners benefit.

Think of your current relationship as a cosmic courtship. The divine spirit seeks your mind and soul in eternal union.

Worship is the conscious and joyous act of recognizing and acknowledging the truth and fact of the intimate and personal relationships of the Creators with their creatures. As the knowledge of the infinite character of the Gods progresses, the act of worship becomes increasingly all-encompassing until it eventually attains the glory of the highest experiential delight and the most exquisite pleasure known to created beings.[9]

If you prove faithful to the trust reposed in you, fusion will eventually ensue. Perfect, eternal, joyful unity with the Divine. But before we reach that moment of union, there is something to understand about what the partnership produces.

4

THE SOUL

You have a body. You have a mind. You have a personality. And within you dwells a fragment of the infinite God.

But there is something else—something that did not exist when you were born, something that is not given but grown, something that neither you nor God could create alone. It exists only because both of you are here, working together, whether you know it or not. It is your soul.

You were designed to be here, designed to develop a mind capable of moral choice, designed to host a fragment of the Divine.

> *Mortal man is not an evolutionary accident. There is a precise system, a universal law, which determines the unfolding of the planetary life plan on the spheres of space.*[1]

And the soul is what that design produces. It is not a poetic metaphor. It is not a vague synonym for your inner life or your deepest feelings. It is an actual reality—a new and distinct creation that emerges from the partnership between your mortal mind and the divine spirit that indwells you. It is, in the most literal sense, their child.

Think about what is being said here. Your mind—material, temporary, evolved from animal origins—is one parent. The divine spirit—eternal, perfect, a fragment of infinite God—is the other parent. And together, through the experience of your life, they are producing something that partakes of both natures but is identical to neither. Your soul is not material. Your body is material; it will return to dust. Your soul is not purely spiritual. The indwelling spirit is purely spiritual; the soul is something else. It occupies a realm between the material and the spiritual, a realm called *morontia*—a word for which there is no earthly equivalent because the reality it describes does not exist on Earth in any form you can observe.

Your soul is the first thing about you that belongs to eternity.

A loom and its fabric. Your mind provides the structure; the spirit weaves the pattern. The result is something beautiful, enduring, and utterly unique—because no one else has your mind, your experiences, your choices. No one else could produce this exact soul; it has never existed before and will never be duplicated.

Your soul does not grow automatically. It is not like your body, which develops whether you attend to it or not. The soul grows through choices—specifically, through choices that have genuine spiritual meaning.

But "choice" may be too deliberate a word for what actually happens. Much of the soul's growth occurs beneath conscious awareness—in the quiet yearning toward something higher, in the instinctive recoil from what is false, in the unnamed pull you feel toward beauty or truth without quite knowing why. You do not always stand at a crossroads and consciously select the higher path. Sometimes you simply want to be better, and that wanting is itself the choice that matters.

> *It is not so much what mind comprehends as what mind desires to comprehend that insures survival; it is not so much what mind is like as what mind is striving to be like that constitutes spirit identification. It is not so much that man is conscious of God as that man yearns for God that results in universe ascension. What you are today is not so important as what you are becoming day by day and in eternity.*[4]

It is not your knowledge that builds your soul. It is your desire. Not what you already understand, but what you are reaching toward. Not who you are at this moment, but who you are becoming. The soul is grown from aspiration as much as from achievement.

This is extraordinarily liberating. It means that your current limitations—your ignorance, your confusion, your failures—do not determine your eternal destiny. What determines it is the direction you are facing. Are you oriented upward? Are you striving to be more than you are? Then your soul is growing, regardless of how far you still have to go.

But it is important to understand what the soul is by understanding what it is not.

The soul is not your conscience. Your conscience is a function of your mind, shaped by culture, upbringing, and experience. It can be wrong. The soul transcends conscience.

The soul is not your emotions. Emotions arise from the interplay of mind and body, and while they can serve spiritual purposes, they are not themselves spiritual realities. Your soul persists after the body and all its emotional machinery ceases to function.

The soul is not your personality. Your personality is the unique pattern of identity bestowed on you by the Universal Father. It is changeless in the presence of change, the one thread of continuity that runs through every phase of your existence.

And the soul is not the indwelling spirit. The spirit is one of its parents, but the soul is a distinct reality.

> *Both the human mind and the divine Adjuster are conscious of the presence and differential nature of the evolving soul—the Adjuster fully, the mind partially.*[5]

So if the soul is none of these things—not conscience, not emotion, not personality, not the spirit—where does it actually develop? The soul grows in the inner life—not in the external world of events and circumstances, but in the interior world of meanings, values, and responses.

> *The advances of true civilization are all born in this inner world of mankind. It is only the inner life that is truly creative.*[6]

Two people can experience the same event and extract entirely different meanings from it. The difference is not in the event but in the inner response—and it is the inner response that builds or diminishes the soul.

This is why external circumstances, however difficult, never have the final word on your destiny. You cannot always control what happens to you, but you always control what you make of it. And what you make of it—the meaning you extract, the values you choose, the character you develop in response—this is the raw material from which your eternal self is being constructed.

Mind is the cosmic instrument on which the human will can play the discords of destruction, or upon which this same human will can bring forth the exquisite melodies of God identification and consequent eternal survival.[7]

Your mind is the instrument. Your will decides what music to play. And the melody or dissonance you produce becomes the character of your soul.

The soul, once initiated, is remarkably resilient. Mistakes and failures can delay its growth, but they cannot destroy it—not as long as you retain even the faintest desire to continue growing.

The mistakes of mortal mind and the errors of human conduct may markedly delay the evolution of the soul, although they cannot inhibit such a morontia phenomenon when once it has been initiated by the indwelling spirit with the consent of the creature will.[8]

This is enormously reassuring. You will stumble. You will fail. You will make choices you regret. But none of these can destroy your soul. Only one thing can end the soul's development: your own final, deliberate, and total rejection of the partnership. As long as some part of you still yearns for something higher, your soul lives and grows.

But there are things that stunt growth. Materialism, the lived conviction that only physical things are real, starves the soul by denying it nourishment. Fear constricts the inner life, narrowing the space in which spiritual growth can occur. Pride deceives, convincing you that you have already arrived when the journey has barely begun. Self-deception corrupts the mind, the very instrument through which the spirit must work.

But perhaps the most subtle threat is simply neglect. The soul that is never attended to, never fed, will remain stunted because it was never cultivated. And yet, even with all these threats, the overall design is not punitive.

The mortal career, the soul's evolution, is not so much a probation as an education. Faith in the survival of supreme values is the core of religion; genuine religious experience consists in the union of supreme values and cosmic meanings as a realization of universal reality.[9]

Your life is not a punishment to endure. It is an education—and the soul is what grows in you as you learn. The moment this becomes real to you, the moment you grasp that what happens in your daily life is being translated into something permanent, everything shifts.

This saving faith has its birth in the human heart when the moral consciousness of man realizes that human values may be translated in mortal experience from the material to the spiritual, from the human to the divine, from time to eternity.[10]

And what you are learning to become is this: an eternal being, capable of surviving death, capable of continuing to grow through ages and universes beyond imagining, capable eventually of standing in the presence of God on Paradise.

The soul is the embryo of that future self. Right now it is incomplete, still developing, still dependent on the material mind for its conscious expression. But it is growing toward a day when it will become the dominant reality of your existence—when the material scaffolding falls away at death and the soul emerges as the true vehicle of your continuing identity.

There is something real, something of human evolution, something additional to the indwelling spirit, which survives death. This newly appearing entity is the soul, and it survives the death of both your physical body and your material mind. This entity is the conjoint child of the combined life and efforts of the human you in liaison with the divine you, the Adjuster. This child of human and divine parentage constitutes the surviving element of terrestrial origin; it is the morontia self, the immortal soul.[11]

When you die, your body returns to the earth. Your material mind ceases. But your soul—carrying your personality, your character, your spiritual achievements, everything of genuine value from your mortal life—persists. It sleeps, held in safekeeping, until the moment of your reawakening on the training worlds that lie beyond death. And there, in a new form suited to a new stage of existence, you continue.

The soul is what makes this possible. Without it, there would be nothing to carry forward. Without the partnership between you and God, there would be no bridge between the life you live now and the life that awaits.

> *What you begin in time you will assuredly finish in eternity—if it is worth finishing.*[12]

That quiet qualification—"if it is worth finishing"—deserves your attention. The soul is not guaranteed. It is grown. It requires your participation, your choices, your willingness. The divine spirit does its part faithfully, unfailingly, with infinite patience. But it cannot build the soul alone. It needs you.

> *Eternal survival of personality is wholly dependent on the choosing of the mortal mind, whose decisions determine the survival potential of the immortal soul. When the mind believes God and the soul knows God, and when, with the fostering Adjuster, they all desire God, then is survival assured.*[13]

Three partners, one shared desire. That is the formula. And it is already at work in you every day. Every meaningful choice adds substance to a reality that will outlast the universe. Every moment of genuine aspiration, every act of sincere love, and every honest encounter with truth, contributes to the most important construction project in your existence: the building of a soul that can carry you into eternity.

The divine spirit is already at work. Your mind is already the loom. The question is simply what you will weave.

Now let's talk about what happens when that creation is complete—
when the soul has grown enough, and the partnership has deepened
enough, that the two become permanently, eternally, irreversibly one.

5

———————

FUSION

Imagine for a moment that you could merge with another person, actually *unite* with them, so that two beings become one being, two wills become one will, while somehow neither is lost in the process.

Impossible, of course. Personalities are by nature distinct, unique, unrepeatable. You cannot truly merge with another human being without losing yourself or them or both.

But fusion with the indwelling spirit is different, because it is prepersonal, waiting for union with a personality to complete it. However, it does present a value and exude a flavor of divinity which is personal in the highest sense. And you, while fully a person, are incomplete in another way: you are finite, temporary, lacking the eternal stability that only union with deity can provide.

> *In the days of the mortal flesh the divine spirit indwells you, almost as a thing apart, in reality an invasion of man by the bestowed spirit of the Universal Father. But in the morontia life the spirit will become a real part of your personality.* [1]

When fusion occurs, these two incompletions meet and become a completion. The prepersonal fragment achieves personhood through you. You achieve eternal stability through it. Neither is lost. Both are enhanced. A new order of being emerges, one that combines humanity and divinity in a union so intimate that separation becomes impossible. It is the personality synthesis of man and the essence of God, the permanent merging of both into something greater than either could be alone.

Nothing in your current experience compares. It is not like a friendship, though it encompasses the deepest friendship. It is not like romantic union, though that might be the nearest human analogy. It is not like spiritual enlightenment, though it includes that. It is entirely new, the creation of a hybrid being who is neither only human nor only divine but irreversibly *both*.

What awaits is a union so complete that the two partners can never afterward be separated or even distinguished. They become eternally and inseparably *one*.

> *When your earthly course in temporary form has been run, you are to awaken on the shores of a better world, and eventually you will be united with your faithful spirit in an eternal embrace. And this fusion constitutes the mystery of making God and man one. No creature, save those who have experienced fusion, can comprehend the true meaning of the actual values which are conjoined when the identity of a creature of time becomes eternally one with the spirit of Paradise Deity.*[2]

And what does this union mean? Even celestial authors struggle to say.

> *Now have these two identities become one. No language in all the universe of universes is adequate to express the significance of this phenomenon of fusion. It defies all logic, and there is nothing in all the spiritual consciousness of the ascending soul more wonderful or*

more glorious than the joining of the mortal child of time with the divine spirit of the eternal Father.[3]

After fusion, you will still be you. Your personality, that unique pattern of identity that makes you you, continues unbroken. You remember your human life. You retain your relationships, your loves, your experiences. You are recognizable to those who knew you before.

But you are also transformed. The limitations that defined your mortal existence are gone. The uncertainties that plagued you are resolved. The gap between who you are and who you know you ought to be finally and completely closes.

You become perfect, not in the sense of having nothing more to learn or experience, but in the sense of being finally *unified*, finally whole, finally free from the internal contradictions and conflicts that characterized your mortal life. And with that freedom comes a joy that runs deeper than any you have ever experienced. That part of God which becomes an eternal part of you contributes the overtones of divinity to your joyous expressions, even your spiritual laughter.

And you become immortal, not merely surviving death, but transcending it so completely that death becomes impossible, unthinkable, a condition that simply no longer applies to your being. Your existence has been rendered eternal by union with an eternal fragment of deity.

> *Ability to comprehend is the mortal passport to Paradise. Willingness to believe is the key to Havona. The acceptance of sonship, cooperation with the indwelling spirit, is the price of evolutionary survival.*[4]

The price is not suffering. Not sacrifice. Not self-denial. The price is cooperation, accepting that you are a child of God and working with the divine presence that makes eternal life possible. This is what fusion costs: your willingness to partner with the Infinite. The question is not whether you are worthy. The question is when.

For most humans, fusion does not occur during mortal life. The limitations of the physical body, the density of material existence, the gradual pace of spiritual maturation in such an environment—all these factors make fusion extraordinarily rare on Earth.

The vast majority of humans who achieve eternal survival do so by dying, awakening in their next phase of existence, and continuing there until, eventually, they reach the point where fusion becomes possible.

But fusion *can* occur during mortal life. It has happened. Not often, but it is possible. And those rare individuals who achieve it experience the extraordinary: they simply *disappear* from mortal view, translated directly from physical existence to the next phase without experiencing death at all.

> *This fusion during physical life instantly consumes the material body; the human beings who might witness such a spectacle would only observe the translating mortal disappear 'in chariots of fire.'[5]*

Their bodies cease to exist. Their material forms dissolve in a flash of energy. And they awaken, already fused, already immortal, in the training worlds that are the next stage of eternal life.

Imagine the moment. A human reaches the final threshold. The alignment completes. And then:

From the outside, witnesses would see only a flash of light, a sudden brilliance, and then nothing. The body simply gone.

But from the inside, from the perspective of the one experiencing it: a rushing sensation of completion, as if every scattered piece of yourself suddenly snapped into place. The spirit you've carried for decades—the quiet presence you learned to sense, then to commune with, then to love—now floods your entire being. There is no boundary anymore between you and it. There never really was, you realize now. You were always becoming this. Every choice, every prayer, every moment of honest self-transcendence was preparation for this instant when the rehearsal ends and the eternal performance begins.

The angels who have guarded you, who have watched your trials, celebrated your victories, and grieved your setbacks, now witness a transformation that never loses its wonder no matter how many times they see it: a mortal becoming immortal. A creature of time stepping into eternity. Their charge, their assignment, their beloved human responsibility, transformed in an instant into a fellow citizen of the cosmos, someone they will know and work alongside forever.

And you, you who were once so small, so limited, so uncertain, now carry infinity within you. Not as a visitor, but as yourself.

How does someone reach this moment? Each person's journey is unique. But broadly speaking, there are certain criteria that are met before fusion takes place.

You are ready when your will and the Father's will have become aligned. You consistently choose truth, beauty, and goodness because you have come to love them, not because you fear punishment or seek reward. Your motivations have become pure. You behave divinely.

You are ready when you have achieved spiritual stability. The swings between faith and doubt, between selflessness and selfishness, between love and fear, have ceased. You have become predictable in your spiritual responses.

You are ready when your soul has developed sufficiently. Remember, your soul is the joint creation of you and God. It must reach a certain level of development—must contain enough spiritual reality, enough experiential wisdom, enough moral character—before fusion can occur.

You are ready when you genuinely desire it. Fusion is not imposed. Even when all other conditions are met, if you hesitate, if you have reservations, if some part of you is not yet ready to take this irreversible step, it will not happen. The Father waits for your whole-hearted assent.

Fusion never occurs until the mandates of the superuniverse have pronounced that the human nature has made a final and irrevocable choice for the eternal career.[6]

When these conditions are met, when the time is right, fusion occurs. And it occurs in an instant. One moment you are a mortal being with an indwelling spirit. The next moment you are a new order of being. You are *Father-fused*.

When mortal man fuses with an actual fragment of the existential Cause of the total cosmos, no limit can ever be placed upon the destiny of such an unprecedented and unimaginable partnership.[7]

6

THE SEVEN CIRCLES

The journey to fusion has a map. Seven circles of spiritual progress, concentric rings of growth that mark your advancement from the outermost reaches of spiritual awareness toward the center where you and the spirit unite.

You began on the outer circle, the seventh, when that divine fragment first took its post in your young mind. You had made your first moral choice, demonstrating the capacity for spiritual response, but you were just beginning. The vast territory of spiritual potential stretched before you, largely unexplored. And you have been traveling inward ever since, whether you cooperated consciously or stumbled forward blindly.

Understanding these circles transforms the vague goal of spiritual growth into reality you can sense, work toward, and eventually attain.

The seven circles do not measure your achievements. They do not track how many good deeds you have performed, how much scripture you have memorized, how many hours you have spent in prayer.

The circles measure deeper realities: your cosmic insight, your capacity to comprehend spiritual reality, your ability to grasp transcendent meanings and values, and your attunement to the divine presence within. And this capacity matters, because God unfailingly manifests himself to every one of his creatures up to the fullness of that creature's ability to spiritually grasp the qualities of divine truth, beauty, and goodness. The circles are not hoops to jump through. They are expansions of your capacity to receive what God is always offering.

> *The psychic circles are not exclusively intellectual; they have to do with personality status, mind attainment, soul growth, and spirit attunement. The successful traversal of these levels demands the harmonious functioning of the entire personality, not merely of some one phase thereof.*[1]

A person can perform religious rituals perfectly yet miss their true meaning entirely. Another person might never enter a church yet possess profound insight into the nature of reality and their relationship with the divine. The circles measure the second quality, not the first.

Circle progress cannot be faked. You cannot perform your way into higher circles. The circles respond to real transformation, to actual changes in who you are, how you perceive, and what you understand. You cannot even pray your way there directly, though prayer creates conditions for transformation.

Most humans are still progressing through the circles when mortal life ends. Growth continues on the mansion worlds. The outer circles represent the early stages of learning to coordinate your human will with divine purposes.

Movement through these outer circles happens as you develop the habit of choosing the higher way. Each time you choose truth over convenience, love over indifference, service over selfishness, you strengthen the connection between your mind and the spirit within. Each choice creates capacity for the next choice. Gradually, almost imperceptibly, you move inward.

The fourth, third, and second circles represent increasingly sophisticated coordination between you and the divine presence within. Here, the partnership deepens. The spirit's influence becomes more perceptible—not as an external voice, but as an internal clarity that guides your thinking and choosing.

> *Circle by circle your intellectual decisions, moral choosings, and spiritual development add to the ability of the indwelling spirit to function in your mind; circle by circle you thereby ascend from the lower stages of association and mind attunement, so that the spirit presence is increasingly able to register its picturization of destiny.*[2]

A remarkable shift happens at the third circle: you receive personal guardianship. Before this point, you shared guardian angels with others. But when you achieve the third circle, a pair of seraphic guardians is assigned exclusively to you. These are actual beings who will accompany you through the remainder of your mortal life and beyond, dedicated to your welfare and advancement.

This assignment recognizes your attainment. You have demonstrated sufficient spiritual stability and potential that the universe invests personal resources in your continued development. You are becoming a recognized citizen of the cosmic community.

The first and innermost circle represents the closest approach a mortal can make to the indwelling spirit while still in the flesh. Here, the partnership has matured to the point where direct communication opens.

> *Though the voice of the spirit presence is ever with you, most of you will hear it seldom during a lifetime. Human beings below the third and second circles of attainment rarely hear the direct voice of the spirit presence except in moments of supreme desire, in a supreme situation, and consequent upon a supreme decision.*[3]

Those on the outer circles rarely hear the spirit's voice except in extreme circumstances. But as you progress inward to the third, second, and first circles, direct communication becomes increasingly possible. The contact that once required crisis becomes accessible in ordinary life.

First-circle mortals have achieved something extraordinary: they have aligned their human nature with divine purposes to such a degree that fusion can occur even during mortal life. Most will still experience fusion after death. But the inner preparation is nearly complete.

You move from circle to circle by the totality of your life choices and the quality of your inner development. And that development follows a natural progression: spiritual growth is first an awakening to needs, next a discernment of meanings, and then a discovery of values. The outer circles are where you recognize that something is missing. The middle circles are where you begin to understand what it means. The inner circles are where you grasp what truly matters, and live accordingly.

The motivation of faith makes experiential the full realization of man's sonship with God, but action, completion of decisions, is essential to the evolutionary attainment of consciousness of progressive kinship with the cosmic actuality of the Supreme Being.[4]

Faith alone is not enough—action must follow. Decisions must be made, life must be lived. Advancement depends on what you do, not only on what you believe or intend.

When you perceive the right course, take it. When insight comes, act on it. When the higher path becomes clear, walk it. Each completed decision creates capacity for the next. Each action taken in alignment with divine purposes strengthens your coordination with the spirit.

The circles also respond to your intellectual development—your growing understanding of cosmic reality, your expanding comprehension of how the universe works and where you fit within it. Study and learning are important. Expanding your mind to contain larger truths creates space for the spirit to work more effectively within you.

And the circles respond to your social development—your capacity for authentic relationships, your ability to love others as the Father loves them, your willingness to serve. Spiritual maturation is not merely private; it expresses itself in how you treat other beings.

Circle progress prepares you for fusion. Each circle attained represents one step closer to the moment when you and the indwelling spirit can unite permanently.

> *The achievement of the seven cosmic circles does not equal fusion. There are many mortals living on the material worlds who have attained their circles, but fusion depends on yet other greater and more sublime spiritual achievements, upon the attainment of a final and complete attunement of the mortal will with the will of God.*[5]

Even first-circle attainment does not guarantee fusion. It requires final and complete attunement of your will with the Father's will. This is not the same as perfect obedience to rules. It is the alignment of your deepest desires with divine purposes—wanting what God wants because you have come to understand that God wants the best for you.

> *The great goal of human existence is to attune to the divinity of the indwelling presence; the great achievement of mortal life is the attainment of a true and understanding consecration to the eternal aims of the divine spirit who waits and works within your mind.*[6]

Though the circles do not guarantee fusion, they do create the conditions for this alignment. They develop your capacity for attunement. They strengthen the connection through which alignment emerges. Without circle progress, fusion cannot occur. With sufficient progress, fusion becomes inevitable—if not during mortal life, then afterward, when the limitations of flesh no longer constrain your growth.

You cannot know precisely which circle you are on. The circles do not come with markers or announcements. But you can sense the general territory.

Are spiritual realities still theoretical concepts you accept on faith? You are likely in the outer circles, still developing the capacity for direct perception.

Do you sometimes sense the presence of something greater within you, guiding your thoughts toward truth? You may be approaching the middle circles, where coordination with the indwelling spirit becomes more conscious.

Do you find that your will increasingly aligns with what you perceive as divine purposes, not from obligation but from genuine desire? You are moving toward the inner circles, approaching the threshold to true immortality.

Wherever you are, the path forward is the same: choose the higher way, complete your decisions, act on your insights, expand your understanding, deepen your relationships, love more fully, serve more willingly, and worship more sincerely.

The circles will respond. The indwelling spirit will register your progress. And step by step, decision by decision, you will move inward toward the center where you and the Divine become one.

> *When the development of the intellectual nature proceeds faster than that of the spiritual, such a situation renders communication with the indwelling spirit both difficult and dangerous. Likewise, overspiritual development tends to produce a fanatical and perverted interpretation of the spirit leadings of the divine indweller. Lack of spiritual capacity makes it very difficult to transmit to such a material intellect the spiritual truths resident in the higher superconsciousness.*[7]

Neither mind nor spirit can advance alone. Intellectual expansion without spiritual development creates barriers. Spiritual enthusiasm without intellectual grounding creates distortion. The ideal is integrated growth—mind and spirit developing together, each supporting the other, both advancing toward the fusion that awaits.

This is the path. These are the circles. And you are already on the journey.

7

THE TRANSFORMATION

What does fusion feel like? This is impossible to fully describe, because it is an experience beyond any human frame of reference. No one who has achieved fusion during mortal life remains to tell about it. Their physical bodies vanish in a flash of spiritual energy, and they awaken transformed in the next phase of existence.

For most, fusion typically occurs beyond death on training worlds prepared for ascending mortals. By that point, the person has undergone significant transformation, shedding material limitations and growing in spiritual capacity. But the exact timing varies enormously based on individual development. Some achieve fusion earlier; some require further development in higher realms. The Father is infinitely patient, and the moment of fusion comes precisely when you are ready—not a moment too soon, not a moment too late.

But we can infer much from the nature of what fusion is.

> *Eternal fusion of the Adjuster with the evolutionary soul of man is the factual experience of eternal union with God as a universe associate of Deity.*[1]

The deepest sense must be of completion, something long-awaited finally occurring, two incomplete realities finally completing each other. It would simply feel right, like coming home after a long and difficult journey, like finding something you didn't even know you had lost.

> *On worlds such as Earth there is a real betrothal with the divine gifts, a life and death engagement. If you survive, there is to be an eternal union, an everlasting fusion, the making of man and spirit one being.*[2]

There would be expansion. Your consciousness would suddenly encompass realities it could never hold before. Not just knowledge, but capacity—capacity to understand, to feel, to perceive. It would be as if your entire being suddenly had more room, more space, more possibility.

There would be recognition. You would finally, fully understand who the indwelling spirit was and what it had been doing all those years. Every moment of divine guidance you half-noticed, every spiritual impulse you followed, every intuition of truth you grasped. You would see it all clearly now, see how patiently and lovingly you were being led toward this moment.

There would be joy—deep, unshakeable joy, independent of external conditions. You would have achieved your destiny. You would have become what you were always meant to become. And the sheer rightness of it would produce joy that eclipses every earthly pleasure you ever experienced.

There would be security. Death would no longer be possible. Not just unlikely, not just avoidable, but impossible. Your state of being would have become eternal, indestructible, permanent. You would never cease to exist. Nothing in the universe could unmake you. This security would be profoundly reassuring.

And finally, overwhelmingly, there would be love—the recognition that you are loved utterly, completely, and eternally by the being who has now become part of you. The love God always felt for you would no longer be hidden or muted or indirect. It would flood your consciousness directly, and you would realize with stunning clarity that you have been loved like this from the beginning, loved with a devotion you never imagined possible.

We can surmise this from understanding what fusion accomplishes and what it means. But the actual experience remains beyond the veil, something we will only know when we ourselves pass through that supernal transformation.

After fusion, everything changes. Not in the sense of becoming alien to your former self, but in the sense of becoming fully, finally who you are.

You cannot die. This is not merely life extension, not merely survival of death. It is the absolute impossibility of ceasing to exist. Your being has been rendered eternal by union with an eternal fragment of deity. The universe itself could end and you would still exist.

Fusion imparts eternal actualities to personality which were previously only potential.[3]

Your capacity grows enormously—your ability to understand, to love, to create, to serve. The limitations that bounded your mortal existence begin to fall away. You can learn more readily, comprehend more deeply, grow more swiftly. You don't suddenly know everything, but your potential for expansion becomes greatly enhanced.

Your perception of spiritual realities expands. While you don't suddenly see all spiritual beings (perception develops progressively through your ascension), you comprehend spiritual truths and divine purposes with a clarity that was impossible before. The spiritual dimension of reality becomes increasingly accessible to your understanding.

You are now a son or daughter of God in the most literal sense, a fused being carrying divinity itself within you. This is not merely honorary status. It is ontological reality. You are transformed.

And nothing can separate you from God now. No failure, no mistake, no cosmic catastrophe can undo what has been done. The partnership is permanent. You and the Divine have become an eternal unity that will continue growing, serving, and experiencing reality together throughout all ages to come.

> *One of the most amazing earmarks of religious living is that dynamic and sublime peace, that peace which passes all human understanding, that cosmic poise which betokens the absence of all doubt and turmoil.*[4]

This peace is not the only gift. Fusion confers specific new endowments: the fixation of divinity quality, meaning your divine nature is now permanently established; access to past-eternity experience and memory; immortality in the absolute sense; and a capacity for growth that extends toward infinity itself. These are not merely spiritual enhancements but concrete new realities of your transformed being.

> *When fusion has been effected, there can be no future danger to the eternal career of such a personality. Celestial beings are tested throughout a long experience, but mortals pass through a relatively short and intensive testing on the material and morontia worlds.*[5]

Morontia is the realm between material and spiritual—the intermediate state where you exist after death but before becoming fully spirit. Your testing happens here and now, in mortal life, and continues on the mansion worlds. Once fusion occurs, the testing is complete. Your loyalty is established forever.

You are a fused son or daughter of the Universal Father. And nothing in all eternity can change that. But fusion does more than secure your personal destiny. It connects you to something far larger.

Through fusion, you become a living part of a phenomenon of gigantic proportions—the growing, evolving Supreme Being who encompasses all finite reality. Your fusion constitutes you as a contributing participant in the cosmic project of bringing the entire universe to perfection. You are no longer merely an observer of divine purposes; you are now an agent of them, forever.

Has the triumphant divine spirit won personality by magnificent service to humanity, or has the valiant human acquired immortality through sincere efforts to achieve godlikeness? It is neither; but they together have achieved the evolution of a member of one of the unique orders of the ascending personalities of the Supreme.[6]

8

COOPERATION

Most people achieve fusion after death. So why cooperate now? Because the person you are now is becoming the person you will be forever. Every choice you make, every thought you think, and every habit you form are shaping your eternal self.

You could drift through life, make minimal spiritual effort, barely cooperate with the divine spirit, and still survive to eternal life. But you would enter eternity as a spiritual infant, requiring extensive remedial work to catch up to where you could have been if you had taken your spiritual life seriously.

Or you could embrace your spiritual development now, cooperate fully with the indwelling presence, make conscious choices toward cosmic maturity, and enter eternity as a relatively mature being, ready for more advanced service, capable of greater joy, positioned for more meaningful experiences.

The time you invest now pays eternal dividends. Every act of worship, every moral choice, every moment of real love—these are investments with infinite returns. They shape who you are becoming, and who you are becoming is who you will be forever. And the heart of it all is simple: the affectionate dedication of your will to the doing of the Father's will. That is your choicest gift to God—in fact, it is the only gift of true value you can offer. Not your talents, not your accomplishments, not your knowledge. Your will, freely and lovingly given.

You don't need to be perfect immediately. Transformation is gradual, developmental, organic. But you do need to *start*. You do need to be moving in the right direction. You do need to be cooperating rather than resisting.

The divine indweller is patient, but life is short. Your mortal years are few. The opportunity to build your soul in these particular conditions, the unique challenges and gifts of material existence, will not come again. Use them well. And do not expect God to make it comfortable.

> *The indwelling spirit is not interested in making the mortal career easy; rather is it concerned in making your life reasonably difficult and rugged, so that decisions will be stimulated and multiplied. These decisions bring about repeated contacts with divinity, and each decision contributes to your eternal growth.* [1]

Consider what is at stake. If you reject this partnership, not through occasional failure or doubt, but through final, deliberate refusal, the spirit that has loved you for a lifetime will return to the Father alone. It will carry with it everything of value from your life, every experience worth preserving. But it will carry these as memories, not as you. The personality that lived those moments will simply end. Not transformed. Not continued elsewhere. Ended. Everything you were, everything you might have become, every relationship, every act of love or courage or beauty, will cease. The spirit will go on. You will not. This is not punishment. It is simply what happens when a soul is never completed, when the mortal partner refuses to finish becoming what they were designed to become.

So how do you get there? How do you cooperate with this process even now, even in your mortal life, to increase the likelihood of fusion and to lay the groundwork for eternal advancement?

Habits which favor religious growth embrace cultivated sensitivity to divine values, recognition of religious living in others, reflective meditation on cosmic meanings, worshipful problem solving, sharing one's spiritual life with one's fellows, avoidance of selfishness, refusal to presume on divine mercy, and living as in the presence of God.[2]

The answer is both simple and demanding: you must choose spiritual reality over material appearance, eternal values over temporary gratification, divine will over selfish impulse, consistently, until these choices become your nature.

The goal of human self-realization should be spiritual, not material. The only realities worth striving for are divine, spiritual, and eternal.[3]

But do not misunderstand what this demands of you.

Cooperation with the divine gift does not entail self-torture, mock piety, or hypocritical and ostentatious self-abasement; the ideal life is one of loving service rather than an existence of fearful apprehension.[4]

Release whatever images you carry of spiritual effort as grim, difficult, punishing. The path to fusion is not paved with suffering. It is paved with love—love given and received, love expressed in service, love lived without fear. If your spiritual practice feels like torture, your approach has gone wrong. But neither is it a technique for attaining a static and blissful peace of mind. It is an impulse for organizing the soul for dynamic service.

So what does that look like? How do you organize your soul for service while living a normal human life?

Start with faith. Living trust in the goodness and purpose of the universe. Faith that reaches beyond proof, that dares to believe in things unseen because they are recognized as true at the deepest levels of intuition and experience. The indwelling spirit can work far more effectively with a mind that trusts than with a mind that constantly doubts, questions, and hedges its bets. Faith opens channels. Skepticism closes them.

The God-knowing soul dares to say, 'I know,' even when this knowledge of God is questioned by the unbeliever. Faith transforms the philosophic God of probability into the saving God of certainty.[5]

Make moral choices consciously. Every day brings countless small decisions. Each one is an opportunity to choose the higher way—to be honest when lying would be easier, to be generous when holding back would be simpler, to be loving when indifference would be safer. These small choices accumulate. They shape your character. They build your soul. The spirit watches every single one, and every choice that aligns with spiritual values is registered, preserved, made part of your eternal self.

Worship regularly. Prayer is asking for things, seeking help. Worship is different. It is communion with divinity for its own sake, simply to acknowledge God, to love and rest in his presence without seeking anything beyond the presence itself. When you worship, the spirit is given maximum opportunity to influence your thinking, to spiritualize your mind, to align your will with divine will.

This choosing of the Father's will is the spiritual finding of the spirit Father by mortal man. If this choice is made, sooner or later will the God-choosing son find inner union with the indwelling God fragment.[6]

Seek truth relentlessly. Actual truth—reality as it is, not as you wish it were. Be willing to abandon cherished beliefs if evidence or insight reveals them as false. Be willing to follow truth wherever it leads, even if it leads to uncomfortable places. The indwelling spirit is truth. It responds powerfully to the love of truth and the desire to align your understanding with reality.

Love people. See them as the Father sees them, recognizing their potential even when they don't recognize it themselves, treating them with the dignity due to beings who also carry divine fragments within them.

You cannot truly love your fellows by a mere act of the will. Love is only born of thoroughgoing understanding of your neighbor's motives and sentiments.[7]

Love is the supreme spiritual reality. When you love truly, when you love unselfishly, you most closely approximate the nature of God. The indwelling spirit works most powerfully through love, because love is its native language.

Serve where you can. Find ways to make the world better, perhaps through your work, or simply being kind and helpful in everyday interactions. Service to others is service to God, because every person you help is a child of the Infinite.

The contact of the mortal mind with its indwelling spirit, while often favored by devoted meditation, is more frequently facilitated by wholehearted and loving service in unselfish ministry to your fellow creatures.[8]

Service is not just morally good; it's spiritually developmental. It gets you outside yourself, breaks the tyranny of self-centeredness, trains you in the outward-focused love that characterizes higher levels of existence.

Study. Learn. Read widely—philosophy, theology, science, history, literature. The more you understand about reality, about human nature, about the universe, the more effectively the spirit can work with your mind. A rich, well-informed, thoughtful mind is a far better instrument for spiritual deepening than an empty or narrow one.

Practice stillness. In the constant noise and activity of modern life, create spaces of quiet—times when you deliberately step back from busyness, turn off distractions, and simply be. In those quiet spaces, the indwelling spirit can communicate more clearly, and you can perceive its presence more distinctly.

Spiritual development depends, first, on the maintenance of a living spiritual connection with true spiritual forces and, second, on the continuous bearing of spiritual fruit.[9]

But do not fall into the trap of excessive introspection or mystical passivity. Spirituality grows through action as much as contemplation.

Accept suffering without bitterness. Life will bring pain, loss, disappointment, failure, and grief. These experiences are not punishments. Nor are they meaningless. They are opportunities for the development of patience and compassion and deeper faith. The way you respond to suffering shapes your character, as does the way you respond to success. The divine monitor can use suffering to spiritualize you, if you let it, if you don't become bitter, if you don't lose faith, if you continue to trust even when everything seems dark.

None of this is easy. If it were easy, everyone would do it. But it is possible, and it can be distilled to four essentials.

You can consciously augment spirit harmony by:

Choosing to respond to divine leading; sincerely basing the human life on the highest consciousness of truth, beauty, and goodness, and then coordinating these qualities of divinity through wisdom, worship, faith, and love.

Loving God and desiring to be like him—genuine recognition of the divine fatherhood and loving worship of the heavenly Parent.

Loving man and sincerely desiring to serve him—wholehearted recognition of the brotherhood of man coupled with an intelligent and wise affection for each of your fellow mortals.

Joyful acceptance of cosmic citizenship—honest recognition of your progressive obligations to the Supreme Being, awareness of the interdependence of evolutionary man and evolving Deity.[10]

One principle, four directions: respond to spirit leading, love God, love people, and accept your place in the cosmos.

9

COMMUNION

You want to hear the divine voice within you. You want clearer guidance, more perceptible direction, a stronger sense of the presence that shares your inner life. This is a legitimate desire.

> *The indwelling spirit unfailingly arouses in man's soul a true and searching hunger for perfection together with a far-reaching curiosity which can be adequately satisfied only by communion with God, the divine source of that spirit.*[1]

But the divine presence is not hiding from you. It is not playing games, withholding contact until you perform the right rituals or achieve some arbitrary level of worthiness. The barriers to deeper communion are on your side, not God's. Understanding these barriers, and the conditions that favor contact, transforms vague spiritual longing into practical headway.

> *The fact of God's presence in creature minds is determined by whether or not they are indwelt by Father fragments, but his effective presence is determined by the degree of cooperation accorded them by the minds of their sojourn.*[2]

This distinction matters. The spirit is present in you. That is settled, unchangeable, a gift you did not earn and cannot lose. But its *effective* presence—how powerfully it can work in your life, how clearly you can perceive its guidance, how deeply you can commune—this depends on you. The gift is given. The connection is developed.

The divine gift operates on a level of reality so purely spiritual that direct perception is extraordinarily difficult for a material mind. You are trying to tune a radio made of stone to frequencies that require crystal.

> *The chief difficulty you experience in contacting with your spirits consists in this very inherent material nature. So few mortals are real thinkers; you do not spiritually develop and discipline your minds to the point of favorable liaison with the divine monitors.* [3]

Your mind is the interface between you and the divine spirit. When that mind is undisciplined—scattered, anxious, pulled in a thousand directions—it cannot register the subtle impressions the spirit is constantly attempting to convey. The spirit speaks, but the noise drowns out the signal.

This is not a moral failing. It is a technical limitation. The material mind was primarily designed for survival in a material world, not necessarily for perceiving spiritual realities. That you can perceive them at all is remarkable. That perception is difficult should surprise no one.

Yet certain conditions make contact more likely. The spirit cannot be manipulated, but certain environments make communication easier.

The connection is reciprocal. Your intentional thoughts, directed inward toward the divine presence, actually reach the spirit. And the spirit responds. You think toward God, God thinks toward you. You talk to God, God talks to you. Your love reaches inward, love returns. This is the exchange that is communion.

What you feel first are the spiritual feelings: joy, peace, love, a warmth that fills you from within. And being in this state elevates your mind. Do not dismiss these experiences as merely psychological. You cannot comprehend the infinitude of God—no finite mind can think through such an absolute reality. But you can actually feel, literally experience, the full and undiminished impact of the infinite Father's love. And that experience does something to you.

Your awareness expands. Your consciousness operates at a higher level. Problems that seemed intractable suddenly reveal solutions. Connections you couldn't see become obvious. Understanding that eluded you arrives without effort. This is not necessarily the spirit sending you messages—it is your mind, temporarily upgraded by contact with the divine, able to perceive what it could not perceive before.

As long as you maintain that higher state, the expanded capacity remains. Your brain activity changes during meditative prayer—this is documented.[4] The mind in communion with the Infinite is simply more capable than the mind operating alone.[5] The insights that come are yours, but they are yours operating at a level you cannot reach without the connection.

Your body responds to communion—it is part of the medium through which spiritual experience becomes perceptible to you.[6] The peace is not merely psychological; it registers in your physiology.[7] The joy has chemical correlates. The love affects your heart, your breathing, your entire organism.[8] This is how embodied beings experience the Divine. The body is the instrument through which the spirit's response becomes perceptible to you. When engaged in communion, the body feels it.

Mental quiet favors these moments—not emptiness, but the reduction of mental noise, the stilling of anxious chatter. This is why meditation helps, why prayer helps, why contemplative practices across all tradi-tions create conditions for insight. They reduce the static that obscures the signal. And sincere seeking matters. The spirit responds to genuine desire for truth, not idle curiosity. When you truly want to know, when you are willing to follow truth wherever it leads, when your seeking is existential necessity rather than intellectual exercise—the spirit can work with this. Half-hearted seeking produces half-hearted results.

There are two forms of communion, and understanding their difference matters.

Prayer is asking. It involves needs, concerns, the desire for guidance or help—whether for yourself or for others. There is nothing wrong with this. The child naturally brings needs to the parent, and the soul that intercedes for others expands its capacity to love. But prayer, however sincere and however unselfish, still centers on need.

Worship is different. Worship forgets the self entirely. It seeks nothing, expects nothing, asks for nothing. It is simply the soul's response to the recognition of God's nature—his beauty, his goodness, his love. And in those moments, something extraordinary happens: the indwelling spirit takes your inexpressible longings, your unutterable aspirations, and communicates them directly to the Father. Your wordless adoration reaches God through the very spirit that dwells within you.

> *Worship is for its own sake; prayer embodies a self- or creature-interest element; that is the great difference between worship and prayer. There is absolutely no self-request or other element of personal interest in true worship; we simply worship God for what we comprehend him to be. Worship asks nothing and expects nothing for the worshiper.*[9]

Think of it this way: in prayer, you are still thinking about need—your own or someone else's. In worship, you forget need entirely. You are absorbed in contemplation of God, not in contemplation of what is lacking.

Prayer is self-reminding—sublime thinking; worship is self-forgetting —superthinking. Worship is effortless attention, true and ideal soul rest, a form of restful spiritual exertion.[10]

Both practices have value. Both contribute to spiritual development. But they accomplish different things. Prayer enriches life. Worship illuminates destiny.

As prayer may be likened to recharging the spiritual batteries of the soul, so worship may be compared to the act of tuning in the soul to catch the universe broadcasts of the infinite spirit of the Universal Father.[11]

Prayer recharges you. It restores your energy, clarifies your thinking, aligns your will with divine purposes. It is active, engaged, directed toward specific outcomes.

Worship tunes you. It opens channels of reception. It allows you to receive what the universe is constantly broadcasting but what you normally cannot hear because you are too busy transmitting. In worship, you stop talking and start listening—not for specific messages, but for the presence itself.

Prayer is the breath of the spirit life in the midst of the material civilization of the races of mankind. Worship is salvation for the pleasure-seeking generations of mortals.[12]

In a world obsessed with getting and having, worship offers something radical: the experience of pure giving, pure appreciation, pure love directed Godward with no expectation of return—yet receiving everything in return.

Prayer is natural. You do not need to learn elaborate techniques. But certain attitudes make prayer more effective—not because God responds differently, but because you become more capable of receiving what God is always offering.

Prayer does not manipulate the universe. It transforms the one who prays. When you pray sincerely, you align yourself with realities larger than your immediate concerns. You open yourself to perspectives you could not access while locked in anxious self-focus. You create internal conditions that make guidance receivable.

Effective prayer requires honesty. You must face your situation as it actually is, not as you wish it were. You must acknowledge your real needs, your real fears, your real desires—even the ones you are ashamed of. God already knows. Pretense accomplishes nothing.

Effective prayer requires owning your responsibilities. Prayer is not a substitute for action. It is not a way to avoid the hard work of solving your own problems. You may rightly seek guidance before you act—but you should not ask God to do what you can do for yourself.

Effective prayer requires faith—not certainty about specific outcomes, but trust in the goodness of the universe and the wisdom of divine purposes. You pray not knowing exactly how your prayer will be answered, trusting that it will be answered in whatever way serves your highest good.

And effective prayer leads somewhere. It does not circle endlessly around the same requests. It moves toward worship—toward moments when you forget your needs entirely and simply rest in the presence of the One you are addressing.

> *Prayer led Jesus up to the supercommunion of his soul with the Supreme Rulers of the universe of universes. Prayer will lead the mortals of earth up to the communion of true worship.*[15]

Worship cannot be commanded or manufactured. It often arises spontaneously when you contemplate the nature of God. But you can create conditions that lead to worship.

Begin with prayer. Address your needs, your concerns, your requests. Get them out of the way. Process the burdens you carry so they do not intrude on what follows.

Then turn your attention entirely to God—to his infinite and perfect nature, his unfailing and inexhaustible love, his eternal and transcendent beauty, his boundless and absolute goodness.

> *Worship is the act of a part identifying itself with the Whole; the finite with the Infinite; the son with the Father; time in the act of striking step with eternity.*[16]

You are not asking for anything now. You are simply appreciating, adoring, loving. You are a child looking at its parent with pure affection, wanting nothing except the parent's presence.

This is harder than it sounds. The mind wants to do something, accomplish something, get something. Worship asks you to stop all of that and simply be—present, attentive, receptive, grateful.

When worship happens—and it may happen only in glimpses at first—something shifts. The stress of life loosens. The fear of isolation dissolves. You feel connected to something vastly larger than yourself, something that holds you, something that will never let you go.

> *The strain of living—the time tension of personality—should be relaxed by the restfulness of worship. The feelings of insecurity*

This is immersion in the deepest reality. And when you return from worship to ordinary life, you return changed—calmer, clearer, more energized, more capable, more loving. The worship itself asked nothing. But it gave everything.

Whether through prayer or worship, communion advances through sincerity.

The keys to the kingdom of heaven are: sincerity, more sincerity, and more sincerity. All men have these keys. Men use them—advance in spirit status—by decisions, by more decisions, and by more decisions.[18]

Each time you turn inward and reach toward the divine presence, you are making a decision—a decision for goodness, for truth, for beauty, for love. Each effort at communion, however brief, is a choice that registers in your soul.

But just as certain conditions favor contact, others actively block it. Fear constricts consciousness, narrows attention, and locks you into survival mode. In this state, the higher circuits through which the spirit operates become inaccessible. You cannot perceive subtle spiritual impressions while your entire system is mobilized for threat response. Anxiety—the chronic, low-grade fear that pervades modern life—creates constant static in consciousness. The worried mind cannot perceive gentle guidance because it is too busy generating worst-case scenarios. Reducing anxiety, through whatever means work for you, directly improves spiritual receptivity.

Preconception blocks contact. When you have already decided what is true, you cannot receive new truth. The spirit may be attempting to expand your understanding, to show you what you haven't considered, to challenge a belief that limits you. But if your mind is closed, the impression cannot land.

Materialism blocks contact—not just the philosophical position but the lived orientation, the assumption that only material things are real, that only measurable outcomes matter, that spiritual realities are only theoretical. This orientation creates a filter that screens out spiritual perception. What you don't believe in, you cannot see.

And self-deception blocks contact. When you lie to yourself, you corrupt the very instrument through which the spirit must work. The mind that deceives itself cannot accurately receive or interpret spiritual impressions. Ruthless self-honesty, painful as it sometimes is, clears channels that self-deception clogs.

Nothing advances contact with the indwelling spirit more than decision-making, genuine choices between higher and lower ways of being.

The success of your indwelling spirit in the enterprise of piloting you through the mortal life and bringing about your survival depends not so much on the theories of your beliefs as upon your decisions, determinations, and steadfast faith. [19]

The spirit cannot be pleased or displeased in the human sense. But your decisions create or destroy conditions for the spirit's work. When you choose truth, you create capacity for receiving more truth. When you choose the higher way, you strengthen channels through which higher guidance can flow.

Do not expect the spirit to make your difficult decisions for you. That would defeat the entire purpose of your existence—the development of authentic character through genuine choice. But as you make these decisions well, as you choose consistently in alignment with truth and love and service, you establish yourself on levels where communion becomes increasingly natural.

Apply this understanding through simple, consistent practice.

Begin each day with intention. Before the noise begins, before the demands arrive, take a moment to orient yourself toward the Divine.

Start with prayer: acknowledge your needs, your concerns, your requests. Then move toward worship: release those concerns and simply appreciate the divinity within. Even a few minutes of this practice sets the tone for the day ahead.

Notice moments of insight throughout the day. When clarity comes, when understanding breaks through, pause. Recognize that this may be the spirit at work. Gratitude for these moments can open doors for more of them.

Make decisions consciously. When you face choices, engage them deliberately. Consider the higher alternative. Ask yourself what truth requires, what love demands, what service suggests. Choose consciously. This is where change happens.

Practice stillness. Even brief moments of mental quiet throughout the day create opportunities for contact. You don't need hours of meditation. You need moments of presence, scattered throughout the busy hours—moments where you shift from prayer to worship, from asking to appreciating, from self-reminding to self-forgetting.

Act on guidance received. When you perceive the right course, take it. When insight comes, act on it. The spirit cannot lead those who will not follow. But this does not mean you must be vigilant every waking moment.

> *You should not regard cooperation with your spirit as a particularly conscious process, for it is not; but your motives and your decisions, your faithful determinations and your supreme desires, do constitute real and effective cooperation.*[20]

The deepest cooperation is the posture of your heart and the orientation of your mind. Your motives, your determinations, and your desires constitute the real partnership. When they are aligned with divine purposes, the spirit can work. When they are not, the most elaborate spiritual practices accomplish little.

The partnership deepens not through effort to force contact but through transformation of character that makes contact natural. As you become the kind of person who seeks truth, loves goodness, and serves others—as these become genuine desires—the spirit's voice becomes clearer, its guidance more perceptible, its presence more real.

This is the path. The path is not easy. But it is open to everyone, and every step forward prepares you for the next.

10

———

THE TECHNIQUE

EVERYTHING YOU HAVE READ SO FAR DESCRIBES WHAT THE INDWELLING spirit is, what it does, and where the partnership leads. But knowing about communion is not the same as experiencing it. This chapter is different. This is not theology. This is not philosophy. This is mechanics—how to make contact with the sacred presence that lives within you.

> *Indirectly and unrecognized the indwelling spirit is constantly communicating with the human subject, especially during those sublime experiences of the worshipful contact of mind with spirit in the superconsciousness.*[1]

The spirit is already communicating. The question is whether you will learn to perceive it. And you can.

The technique is simple. But simple does not mean passive. What follows requires real spiritual and energetic effort, the exertion of faculties you may not have names for. You will be making it happen, not merely waiting for it to happen to you.

Begin by closing your eyes. This reduces external input, making it easier to turn attention inward. You are not trying to see anything.

66

You are trying to feel your way toward what that has been there all along.

Speak inwardly to the presence you know dwells within. No formal words are required—simply acknowledge that you are turning toward the divine. You might think: *I'm here. I'm turning toward you.*

Now move your attention inward and downward, away from the chatter of surface thoughts, toward the deepest interior sense you can locate. For many, this feels like a region somewhere between the upper spine and the back of the head. This may also be sensed as being in the central focal point between the heart and mind. It can be perceived as an activation of the energetic centers in the heart, throat and head.

Your experience may differ. Find the place that seems to be the center of your inner being. Go to the deepest place you can reach, beneath the noise, beneath the mental activity, to the quiet core, to the literal center of you. It's simply a shift in attention.

And once you arrive, recognize what is waiting for you there. This divine gift loves you. It is a reality you can feel. This spirit has always loved you. It is loving you now. Let this recognition settle.

The response comes as a warmth that has no physical source, a peace that descends without reason, a quiet joy that fills you from somewhere you cannot name. This is the indwelling spirit responding to your attention. You have turned toward it, and it meets you.

When you feel this response, even faintly, return the love. Think the words if they help: *I love you. I appreciate you. Thank you for being here with me.* But do not merely think them. Feel love toward the presence as you think them. Mean it. Direct affection inward, toward the divine at your center.

Notice what happens. The joy and peace you received now amplify. The love you sent out returns multiplied. The circuit is complete, energy flows in both directions, each exchange deepens the connection.

Continue. Give again. Receive again. The exchange builds. This is neither visualization nor imagination. This is actual communion, the indwelling spirit and your conscious self meeting in the only place where meeting is possible: the interior sanctuary of your own heart and mind.

The practice is a continuous loop. You receive love, you give love, you receive more, you give more. Back and forth, each cycle deepening the connection. *I love you.* Give. Mean it. *You love me.* Receive. Feel it. *I love you.* Give more. *You love me.* Receive more.

The loop has no required endpoint. You can continue as long as you have time and energy. You may eventually experience it as a singular expression rather than a back and forth. Simply expressing your affection, with your attention on your inner being where God dwells, begets an experience where it is difficult to discern who is doing the speaking and who is doing the listening.

Some sessions last seconds, a brief touch of communion in the middle of a busy day. Others extend for many minutes, the exchange deepening until you lose track of time entirely.

Eventually the connection plateaus or external demands intrude. You do not need to close the session formally. Simply carry the peace with you as you return to ordinary awareness. The presence remains. Only your conscious attention shifts.

The phrases you use matter less than the energy you bring to them. Think of words as vehicles—what matters is what you pour into them: your attention, your feeling, your desire to connect.

For giving, you might think: *I love you. I want to know you. Thank you for being here. I choose you.* For receiving: *You love me. You're here with me. You know me completely. You've never left.* You can ask questions, opening yourself to whatever arises: *What do you want me to know? How do you see me? What are we becoming together?*

The response to questions may come as a thought that feels different from your usual thinking—simpler, clearer, more loving. Or as a shift in feeling. Or as silence that somehow communicates. The spirit speaks in impressions, not sentences. Your task is to ask, then listen with your whole being.

But remember: the words are scaffolding. They help aim your consciousness. The actual communion happens at the spiritual level—mind to mind, feeling to feeling. You could think *I love you* a thousand times and feel nothing if the words remain mere words. Or you could think it once, meaning it fully, and feel the response immediately.

What you pour into the words—your love, your reaching—that is what the spirit receives. And what it sends back is energy laced with spiritual meaning: waves of peace, currents of joy, a presence that fills you from within. The heart center can receive a surge of love, the literal force-power of the universal energy of affection.

The experience is difficult to describe directly, but not impossible to evoke.

The circuit. Imagine an electrical circuit with a gap. Power is available but nothing flows because the circuit is incomplete. When you turn your attention inward and reach toward the presence, you close the gap. Current begins to flow. And unlike physical circuits, this one amplifies with use: the more love you send, the more it flows back.

The well. There is a well at the center of your being, deeper than you knew you went. Most days you walk past it, busy with surface matters. But when you stop, approach the edge, and drop in a word of love or a feeling of gratitude, a response comes back up. Living water that fills you. The well is bottomless. The water is inexhaustible. You only have to keep drawing.

Breathing. Inhale: give love, feel it flow toward the inner presence. Exhale: receive love, feel it fill you. Inhale, give more. Exhale, receive more. It becomes as natural as breathing—because it is, in a sense, spiritual respiration. You were designed for this exchange. You have been holding your breath your whole life.

The fire. You have been cold for so long you forgot what warmth felt like. Now you approach a fire, not with effort, just by turning toward it. Warmth touches you. You lean closer. More warmth. You open your hands toward the flames. The heat penetrates deeper. You are not doing anything except positioning yourself to receive what the fire freely gives. The divine presence is like this—always burning, always radiating love. Your only task is to stop turning away.

The embrace. You reach inward, tentatively, like reaching toward someone you hope will embrace you back. And arms you cannot see fold around you. You feel held. You tighten your embrace in response, and the holding deepens. You let yourself be held more fully, and the arms draw you closer still. There is no end to how close you can get, no limit to how fully you can be held.

The dance. It is not a performance where one moves and the other watches. It is a dance—you step, the spirit responds, you respond to the response, and soon you are moving together in a rhythm neither imposed but both created. The better you know your partner, the more effortless the dance becomes. Eventually you stop thinking about steps. You simply move together.

Different metaphors resonate for different people. Find the one that helps you understand what you are reaching for. But whichever image speaks to you, understand that this practice is not passive. You are not simply opening yourself and waiting for God to do all the work. You are actively participating—reaching inward, generating love, sustaining attention, returning affection. This requires effort.

Today you are passing through the period of the courtship of your indwelling spirit; and if you only prove faithful to the trust reposed in you by the divine spirit who seeks your mind and soul in eternal union, there will eventually ensue that morontia oneness, that supernal harmony, that cosmic co-ordination, that divine attunement, that celestial fusion, that never-ending blending of identity, that oneness of being which is so perfect and final that even the most experienced personalities can never segregate or recognize as separate identities the fusion partners—mortal man and divine spirit.[2]

Courtship. The word is precise. You are being wooed by infinity. And courtship requires participation from both parties—attention, responsiveness, the gradual building of intimacy. This is what you are learning.

But it is not physical effort. It is intellectual, energetic, and spiritual effort—the exertion of subtle faculties you may not have known you possessed. The effort of meaning it when you direct love inward. The effort of staying in the deep place when your attention wants to scatter. The effort of allowing feeling rather than merely thinking about feeling.

Think of the difference between listening to music and singing. Listening is receptive. Singing requires you to generate sound, sustain it, put energy into it. Communion is singing and listening. You are not just a passive receiver waiting for God to fill you. You are an active participant, generating love and directing it inward, receiving what comes back, and generating more in response.

Do not be surprised if you feel spent after worshipful communion—more pleasantly tired than depleted, the way you feel after meaningful conversation or satisfying work. You have expended real energy.

Over time, the effort changes. The spiritual muscles strengthen with use. What once required significant exertion becomes more natural. But it never becomes entirely effortless—you are always actively participating, always contributing to the exchange. What changes is that you develop greater capacity. You can go deeper, stay longer, exchange more. The effort decreases as your ability increases. Both happen together.

Your first attempts may produce little. Or they may overwhelm you. The indwelling spirit has been waiting for your attention—some people feel the response immediately and powerfully. Others must practice before the connection becomes perceptible.

If nothing seems to happen, do not conclude that nothing is happening. The spirit is responding. You are simply not yet able to perceive the response. Continue. The faculty develops with use. What is imperceptible today may become obvious tomorrow.

Over time, expect easier access to the deep place, quicker recognition of the spirit response, a stronger sense of the love that meets you, longer and deeper exchanges, and a growing background sense of connection that persists beyond formal practice.

There may be days when the connection seems blocked, when you cannot find the deep place, when God feels distant. This does not mean you have failed. It does not mean the spirit has left. The divine presence remains constant. Your ability to perceive it fluctuates with your state—your tiredness, your stress, your preoccupations. On these days, simply practice as best you can. Even unsuccessful attempts strengthen the faculty you are developing.

A few mistakes are common.

Trying to manufacture feelings—the joy and peace are received, not produced. You generate love to send inward; you receive what comes back. If you try to create the response yourself, you will only create a simulation. Wait for the real thing. It feels different—it arises from a depth beyond your own emotional machinery.

Talking at God instead of with God. This is not monologue prayer. You are not transmitting into a void. You are exchanging with a presence that responds. Pause. Receive. The dialogue is the point.

Expecting words. The spirit does not typically speak in human language as we understand it. It communicates in impressions, meanings, feelings, shifts of awareness. If you are listening for an audible voice, you might miss the response that is coming.

Giving up too quickly. The first minute may be just settling in. If you stop too soon, you never reach the depth where connection happens. Give it time.

Forcing instead of allowing. Effort is required, but not strain. You are reaching, not grasping. Gentle persistence works. Desperate forcing blocks. If you notice yourself straining, relax slightly. Maintain intention without tension.

The practice is not an end in itself. It is training for continuous communion—a state where the connection with the indwelling spirit becomes the background hum of your life rather than a special activity you occasionally perform.

> *These indwelling spirits are loving leaders, your safe and sure guides through the dark and uncertain mazes of your short earthly career; they are the patient teachers who so constantly urge their subjects forward in the paths of progressive perfection. I wish you could love them more, cooperate with them more fully, and cherish them more affectionately.*[3]

Love them more. Cooperate more fully. Cherish more affectionately. This is instruction. The technique you are learning is simply a means by which this loving, cooperating, and cherishing can happen.

As you practice, the sense of presence persists. You finish formal communion and return to ordinary activity, but something remains. A subtle awareness. A quiet companionship. The presence you touched intentionally becomes perceptible unintentionally. You start noticing it at unexpected moments, because it has become familiar enough to recognize.

Living partnership begins here. The indwelling spirit has always been guiding you, but now you feel the guidance as it happens. A gentle pull toward one choice over another. A quiet caution when you are about to err. An inexplicable peace that arrives when you need it. You are not imagining this. You are perceiving what was always occurring but previously went unnoticed.

The practice of communion becomes the foundation for the partnership that leads to fusion. You are learning to work with a divine fragment that will one day be fully you. Every exchange now prepares you for the union that awaits. Every moment of connection strengthens the bond that will become eternal.

The technique is simple: go inward, find the presence, receive love, give love, continue. It is the most important relationship you will ever have—the partnership with divinity itself.

Turn inward. Divinity is waiting. It has always been waiting.

Begin.

11

EFFECTIVE PRAYER

Not all prayer is equally effective. This is not because God responds differently to different prayers, but because the one praying becomes more or less capable of receiving what God is always offering.

This chapter explores what makes prayer effective, offers practical touchpoints for staying connected through busy hours, and closes with prayers from other inhabited worlds—examples of how beings across the universe have expressed their reaching toward the same Father.

The technique described in the previous chapter is the heart of communion—the deep, sustained contact that transforms you over time. Think of it as your anchor practice. Think of what follows as tools and inspiration for extending that communion throughout your days.

Effective prayer is:

Unselfish—not alone for oneself. Prayer that never ventures beyond your own needs remains spiritually cramped. When you pray for others—for their growth, their healing, their awakening—something opens in you. The heart that reaches outward makes room to receive more. This doesn't mean your personal needs are unworthy of prayer; it means they shouldn't be the only subject of your prayers. The soul that habitually intercedes for others develops a capacity for love that purely self-focused prayer cannot produce. You become more like the Father, whose love pours out endlessly toward all his children.

Believing—according to faith. Prayer without faith is like speaking into a disconnected telephone. You must genuinely believe that God hears, that he cares, and that prayer is effective. This doesn't mean you must feel certain of a specific outcome—that would be presumption, not faith. Rather, it means approaching God with confident expectation that he is real, that he is good, and that communion with him changes things. Doubt-filled prayer defeats itself, not because God punishes skepticism, but because a divided mind cannot truly receive. Come to God believing that he wants to give you good things—because he does.

Sincere—honest of heart. God cannot be fooled, and he cannot be impressed by fine words. He sees past every pretense to the true condition of your heart. Therefore, bring him your actual self: your real challenges, your true desires, your sincere doubts. Performative prayer, offered to sound spiritual or to satisfy religious obligation, accomplishes nothing. The Father delights in raw honesty, even when that candor includes confusion or complaint. A sincere cry of "I don't understand" reaches heaven faster than an eloquent prayer recited without feeling. Come as you are.

Intelligent—according to light. Pray with the understanding you have. If you know that God doesn't override human will, don't ask him to force someone to change. If you understand that spiritual growth matters more than material comfort, don't treat God as a cosmic vending machine for physical goods. Intelligent prayer aligns itself with what you know of divine law and cosmic reality. This doesn't mean you need theological expertise, it means you should use the light you've been given. As your understanding grows, your prayers will mature. Pray at the level of your insight, and your insight will deepen.

Trustful—in submission to the Father's all-wise will. This is the crown of all prayer: the willingness to release your grip on outcomes. "Thy will be done" is not resignation but liberation, the recognition that an all-loving, all-knowing Father might have something better in mind than what you've imagined. Trustful prayer says, "I bring you my desire, but I trust your wisdom more than my own." This surrender is not passive; it is the most active faith possible. It declares that you believe God is both good and wise, that his plans for you exceed your limited vision. When you can truly pray this way, you have entered the secret of peace.

> *Such a creature choice is not a surrender of will. It is a consecration of will, an expansion of will, a glorification of will, a perfecting of will; and such choosing raises the creature will from the level of temporal significance to that higher estate wherein the personality of the creature son communes with the personality of the spirit Father.*[1]

These are not arbitrary requirements. They describe the internal conditions that make reception possible. Selfishness closes channels that unselfishness opens. Doubt creates static that faith clears. Insincerity corrupts the very instrument through which guidance must come.

> *The earnest and longing repetition of any petition, when such a prayer is the sincere expression of a child of God and is uttered in faith, no matter how ill-advised or impossible of direct answer, never fails to expand the soul's capacity for spiritual receptivity.*[2]

Even when a prayer seems to go unanswered, even when you ask for something that cannot be granted, the act of sincere prayer itself expands your capacity for spiritual receptivity and changes you in beneficial ways.

> *Prayer is the sincere and longing look of the child to its spirit Father; it is a psychologic process of exchanging the human will for the divine will. Prayer is a part of the divine plan for making over that which is into that which ought to be.*[3]

Prayer is not about convincing God to do what you want. It is about aligning yourself with what God wants, and discovering in the process that what God wants is better than what you were asking for.

> *Prayer and its associated worship is a technique of detachment from the daily routine of life, from the monotonous grind of material existence. It is an avenue of approach to spiritualized self-realization and individuality of intellectual and religious attainment.*[4]

In a life crowded with demands, prayer creates space. It lifts you out of the grind, reminds you what's important, and reconnects you to realities that the urgent obscures.

> *Prayer is an antidote for harmful introspection.*[5]

When you are caught in loops of self-criticism, anxiety, or obsessive analysis, prayer breaks the cycle. It redirects attention from self to God—and in that redirection, the self finds relief.

And much of that self-criticism dissolves when you remember the fact that sonship is a gift. No child has anything to do with earning the status of son or daughter.

> *The earth child comes into being by the will of its parents. Even so, the child of God comes into grace and the new life of the spirit by the will of the Father in heaven. You earn righteousness—progressive character development—but you receive sonship by grace and through faith.*[6]

You do not pray to earn God's love. You already have it. You pray because you are loved, and because prayer is how children naturally communicate with divine parents who love them.

Theory becomes real through practice. Here are some ways to incorporate communion into your daily life.

Morning Orientation. Before rising, before the day's demands arrive, pause. Close your eyes. Acknowledge the presence within.

You might say silently: "You are here. I am here. We begin this day together."

Bring to mind anything you're anxious about—the meeting, the conversation, the task you're dreading. Don't try to solve it. Just acknowledge it. Then release it: "I place this in your hands. Help me see what I need to see."

Now shift from request to appreciation. Think of one thing you're grateful for—something simple, something real. Let that gratitude expand. Feel it in your body.

Rest there briefly.

Open your eyes. The day can begin.

Midday Pause. Somewhere in the middle of your day, stop. This can happen anywhere—at your desk, in your car, walking between appointments.

Take three slow breaths. With each exhale, release tension you didn't know you were holding.

Turn your attention inward. The divine presence is still there. It has been working while you were busy.

Ask: "Is there anything I need to notice? Anything I'm missing?"

Wait. Don't force an answer. If something surfaces, acknowledge it. If nothing surfaces, that's fine too.

Return to your day. But return different—recalibrated, reconnected.

Prayer Practice. When you need to bring something specific to God—a problem, a decision, a burden—this structure helps.

Sit quietly. Breathe until your body settles.

Begin with honesty. What do you actually need? Not what you think you should need—what you actually need. Name it, silently or aloud. God already knows. Pretense wastes time.

Ask yourself: Have I done what I can do? You bring to God the problems that remain after you have exhausted your own resources, not before.

Now bring the need to God. Not as a demand or a bargain, but as a child to a parent. "I need help with this. I don't know what to do. I'm willing to follow guidance if you'll show me."

Wait. Don't rush to fill the silence. Sit with not-knowing. The answer may not come now. It may come tomorrow, or next week, or through another person, or through circumstances you couldn't have predicted. But the asking changes you. It opens channels.

When you feel ready, shift toward appreciation. Let the prayer become worship. Release the need—not because it doesn't matter, but because you've placed it in hands larger than your own.

Rest in God's presence. This is where prayer leads when it goes deep enough.

At Moments of Choice. When facing a significant choice—ethical, relational, vocational—pause before acting. The spirit cannot make your decisions for you, but it can illuminate them.

Ask yourself: What does truth require here? Not what is convenient. Not what avoids conflict. What is actually true about this situation?

Ask: What does love suggest? If I were acting from love rather than fear, what would I do?

Ask: What would serve others? Not just me—what would genuinely help the people affected by this choice?

Notice your resistance. What are you afraid of? What are you protecting? Sometimes the resistance itself reveals what you need to know.

Ask: Which choice would I be proud of in ten years? Which choice aligns with who I want to become?

Then choose. Act. Don't second-guess. The spirit works through your sincere decisions, not through endless deliberation. A wrong decision made sincerely teaches more than a right decision never made.

Moments of Beauty. When beauty stops you—a sunset, a piece of music, a child's laughter, unexpected kindness—don't rush past it.

Pause. Receive it fully. Let it land.

Beauty is a revelation of divine reality. It is not separate from your spiritual life; it is part of it. The capacity to perceive beauty is itself a gift of the spirit.

Say silently: "Thank you for this." Mean it.

Then carry it with you. Let the beauty become fuel for the rest of your day.

Service as Communion. Some of the most powerful moments of contact come not in quiet meditation but in active service, when you forget yourself entirely in caring for another.

When you find yourself serving—helping, listening, giving—bring awareness to what is happening.

Notice when your ego steps aside. Notice when love flows unimpeded. These are moments when the Divine can work through you most powerfully.

You don't need to make these moments spiritual. They already are. You just need to notice.

Evening Review. Before sleep, review the day. Not to judge yourself—to notice, to learn, to grow.

Where did you feel connected to the presence within today? What circumstances made that connection easier? More of that tomorrow.

Where did you feel disconnected? What pulled you away? Not to feel guilty—to understand.

Was there a moment when you chose the higher way—when you could have been petty but weren't, could have lied but didn't, could have ignored someone's need but chose to help? Acknowledge it. This is who you are becoming.

Was there a moment when you chose the lower way? Acknowledge it without shame. Shame doesn't help. What would you do differently? That recognition is the growth. The failure was not wasted.

Release the day. It is complete. Whatever you did or didn't do, it's finished. Tomorrow you begin again, and the spirit will be there when you wake—patient, present, ready to continue the work.

The Sabbath Practice. Once a week, or however often you want, set aside extended time for deeper communion. This is your anchor, the practice that keeps everything else centered.

Use the technique described in the previous chapter. Or simply sit in the presence without structure, letting worship arise as it will. Soft, beautiful music can help quiet the mind and open the heart.

This is not an obligation. It is not a religious duty performed to satisfy a demanding God. It is time with someone who loves you, someone who has been waiting all week for this unhurried meeting.

Come to it not as a task but as a gift—a gift to yourself and a gift to God.

These practices are suggestions, not requirements. Experiment. Adapt them to your life, your temperament, your circumstances. What matters is not the form but the intention—repeated turning toward the inner sanctuary, scattered throughout your days, until the turning becomes natural, until the presence becomes constant, until the partnership becomes unbreakable.

The universe of universes contains countless inhabited worlds, and just as on Earth, these other mortals have learned to pray. These prayers come from other worlds, but they exhibit the same reaching toward the same Father.

They are offered here not as formulas to recite but as examples of how others have expressed what you may struggle to put into words. Use them if they help. Adapt them. Or let them inspire your own.

> *Our Father in whom consist the universe realms,*
>
> *Uplifted be your name and all-glorious your character.*
>
> *Your presence encompasses us, and your glory is manifested*

Imperfectly through us as it is in perfection shown on high.

Give us this day the vivifying forces of light,

And let us not stray into the evil bypaths of our imagination,

For yours is the glorious indwelling, the everlasting power,

And to us, the eternal gift of the infinite love of your Son.

Even so, and everlastingly true.[7]

Our creative Parent, who is in the center of the universe,

Bestow upon us your nature and give to us your character.

Make us sons and daughters of yours by grace

And glorify your name through our eternal achievement.

Your adjusting and controlling spirit give to live and dwell within us

That we may do your will on this sphere as angels do your bidding in light.

Sustain us this day in our progress along the path of truth.

Deliver us from inertia, evil, and all sinful transgression.

Be patient with us as we show loving-kindness to our fellows.

Shed abroad the spirit of your mercy in our creature hearts.

Lead us by your own hand, step by step, through the uncertain maze of life,

And when our end shall come, receive into your own bosom our faithful spirits.

Even so, not our desires but your will be done.[8]

Our perfect and righteous heavenly Father,

This day guide and direct our journey.

Sanctify our steps and coordinate our thoughts.

Ever lead us in the ways of eternal progress.

Fill us with wisdom to the fullness of power

And vitalize us with your infinite energy.

Inspire us with the divine consciousness of

The presence and guidance of the seraphic hosts.

Guide us ever upward in the pathway of light;

Justify us fully in the day of the great judgment.

Make us like yourself in eternal glory

And receive us into your endless service on high.[9]

Our Father who is in the mystery,

Reveal to us your holy character.

Give your children on earth this day

To see the way, the light, and the truth.

Show us the pathway of eternal progress

And give us the will to walk therein.

Establish within us your divine kingship

And thereby bestow upon us the full mastery of self.

Let us not stray into paths of darkness and death;

Lead us everlastingly beside the waters of life.

Hear these our prayers for your own sake;

Be pleased to make us more and more like yourself.

At the end, for the sake of the divine Son,

Receive us into the eternal arms.

Even so, not our will but yours be done.[10]

Glorious Father and Mother, in one parent combined,

Loyal would we be to your divine nature.

Your own self to live again in and through us

By the gift and bestowal of your divine spirit,

Thus reproducing you imperfectly in this sphere

As you are perfectly and majestically shown on high.

Give us day by day your sweet ministry of brotherhood

And lead us moment by moment in the pathway of loving service.

Be you ever and unfailingly patient with us

Even as we show forth your patience to our children.

Give us the divine wisdom that does all things well

And the infinite love that is gracious to every creature.

Bestow upon us your patience and loving-kindness

That our charity may enfold the weak of the realm.

And when our career is finished, make it an honor to your name,

A pleasure to your good spirit, and a satisfaction to our soul helpers.

Not as we wish, our loving Father, but as you desire the eternal good of your mortal children,

Even so may it be.[11]

Our all-faithful Source and all-powerful Center,

Reverent and holy be the name of your all-gracious Son.

Your bounties and your blessings have descended upon us,

Thus empowering us to perform your will and execute your bidding.

Give us moment by moment the sustenance of the tree of life;

Refresh us day by day with the living waters of the river thereof.

Step by step lead us out of darkness and into the divine light.

Renew our minds by the transformations of the indwelling spirit,

And when the mortal end shall finally come upon us,

Receive us to yourself and send us forth in eternity.

Crown us with celestial diadems of fruitful service,

And we shall glorify the Father, the Son, and the Holy Influence.

Even so, throughout a universe without end.[12]

Our Father who dwells in the secret places of the universe,

Honored be your name, reverenced your mercy, and respected your judgment.

Let the sun of righteousness shine upon us at noontime,

While we beseech you to guide our wayward steps in the twilight.

Lead us by the hand in the ways of your own choosing

And forsake us not when the path is hard and the hours are dark.

Forget us not as we so often neglect and forget you.

But be you merciful and love us as we desire to love you.

Look down upon us in kindness and forgive us in mercy

As we in justice forgive those who distress and injure us.

May the love, devotion, and bestowal of the majestic Son

Make available life everlasting with your endless mercy and love.

May the God of universes bestow upon us the full measure of his spirit;

Give us grace to yield to the leading of this spirit.

By the loving ministry of devoted seraphic hosts

May the Son guide and lead us to the end of the age.

Make us ever and increasingly like yourself

And at our end receive us into the eternal Paradise embrace.

Even so, in the name of the bestowal Son

And for the honor and glory of the Supreme Father.[13]

These prayers come from worlds vastly different from your own—worlds with different histories, different challenges, different ways of understanding the cosmos. Yet in every one, you hear the same longing: to know the Father, to do his will, to grow toward perfection, to be received at the end into the eternal embrace.

You are not alone in this journey. Across creation, beings are reaching toward the same God who reaches toward you. The practices in this chapter can be your way of joining that reaching.

What matters more than exercises or formulas is the orientation of your heart, the sincerity of your seeking, and the consistency of your turning toward the divine presence within.

Begin where you are. Use what helps. Discard what doesn't. The spirit will work with whatever you give it.

And over time—through morning orientations and evening reviews, through prayers offered and decisions made, through moments of beauty received and service rendered—you will find that the distance between you and the Divine has narrowed. Not because God moved closer. He was always there. But because you finally learned to notice.

12

THE ASCENT

FUSION IS NOT THE DESTINATION. IT IS THE BEGINNING OF A JOURNEY SO vast that your mortal imagination cannot hold it. What follows is the briefest sketch of where you are going—from the training worlds relatively near your native planet to the very center of all reality.

You awaken after death in resurrection halls on the first of seven mansion worlds, training spheres orbiting a satellite of your system's headquarters. Here you resume your education at exactly the level where death interrupted it. Your body is new, composed of a substance neither purely material nor purely spiritual, but your personality is continuous. You are unmistakably yourself. Those who died before you are here, waiting. The reunion is everything you hoped.

> *Throughout all eternity you will recall the profound memory impressions of your first witnessing of these resurrection mornings.*[1]

The mansion worlds address your deficiencies—biological, intellectual, spiritual. Each sphere has a specific purpose. The first corrects what mortality denied you. The second resolves the mental conflicts that sabotaged your mortal life. The third introduces you to true

90

culture and social harmony. The fourth reveals your place in the larger cosmos. The fifth awakens genuine cosmic consciousness. The sixth often brings fusion for those who have not yet achieved it. The seventh prepares you for citizenship beyond the training spheres. You proceed at your own pace, learning, growing, becoming more than you were.

From sphere to sphere you grow less material, more intellectual, and slightly more spiritual. You are becoming universe minded. This is indeed a time of expanding horizons. It is beginning to dawn upon the enlarging minds of the ascending mortals that some stupendous and magnificent, some supernal and divine, destiny awaits all who complete the progressive Paradise ascension, which has been so laboriously but so joyfully and auspiciously begun.[2]

After the mansion worlds, you graduate to the system headquarters, a vast architectural sphere one hundred times the size of Earth. Here you learn cosmic citizenship, participate in representative government, and gain parental experience if you lacked it in mortality. You meet beings from hundreds of other worlds.You begin to understand that your native planet was one world among millions, and your life on it was only the first chapter. You are no longer merely a survivor of death. You are a cosmic citizen.

If I only had words to tell you of the morontia counterparts of the marvelous physical equipment of the system capital! If I could only go on to portray the sublime grandeur and exquisite perfection of the spiritual appointments of this headquarters world! Your most imaginative concept of perfection of beauty and repleteness of appointment would hardly approach these grandeurs. And it is but the first step on the way to the supernal perfection of Paradise beauty.[3]

The constellation worlds follow—seventy major spheres where you master group ethics, learning to live joyfully with beings utterly unlike yourself. This is the most settled period of your morontia career. The gardens here surpass anything you have seen.

If you enjoy the flowers, shrubs, and trees of Earth, then will you feast your eyes upon the botanical beauty and the floral grandeur of the supernal gardens of the constellation. But it is beyond my powers of description to undertake to convey to the mortal mind an adequate concept of these beauties of the heavenly worlds. Truly, eye has not seen such glories as await your arrival on these worlds of the mortal-ascension adventure.[4]

And the beauty is not only in the gardens. It is in the beings who live there. The permanent citizens, the univitatia, become your training partners. You learn that tolerance is insufficient—you must achieve genuine delight in diversity. When you leave, you carry this capacity forever.

Then comes the local universe capital, where the Creator Son and Creative Spirit who made this entire region of space actually dwell. Here you encounter beings from thousands of worlds, all ascending the same path. You begin to grasp what it means to belong to a universe—not as an observer but as a participant in its purposes. The parochialism of your mortal perspective finally dissolves. You are one note in a symphony of billions, and the symphony is beautiful.

Your passage through this wonderful borderland life will be an unforgettable experience, a charming memory. It is the evolutionary portal to spirit life and the eventual attainment of creature perfection by which ascenders achieve the goal of time, the finding of God on Paradise.[5]

And the transformation required to reach that goal is substantial. From the time you leave material existence until you are constituted a first-stage spirit, you undergo 570 separate and ascending changes in your form and nature. 8 of these occur on the mansion worlds, 71 in the constellation training spheres, and 491 during your sojourn at the headquarters of your local universe. Each change represents growth, refinement, and increasing capacity for spiritual reality. You are being gradually transformed from a being of material origin into a being of spirit destiny.

> *The Gods do not transform a creature of gross animal nature into a perfected spirit by some mysterious act of creative magic. When the Creators desire to produce perfect beings, they do so by direct and original creation. Always the morontia transition intervenes between the mortal estate and the subsequent spirit status.*[6]

Beyond your local universe lies the superuniverse, a realm containing one hundred thousand local universes like your own.

> *The superuniverse is illuminated and warmed by more than ten trillion blazing suns. These suns are the stars of your observable astronomic system. More than two trillion are too distant and too small ever to be seen from Earth. But there are as many suns as there are glasses of water in the oceans of your world.*[7]

You traverse its minor and major sectors, stopping at hundreds of training worlds. Your consciousness expands to hold realities that would have shattered your mortal mind.

> *The headquarters your superuniverse is immediately surrounded by the seven higher universities of advanced spiritual training for ascending will creatures. Each of these seven clusters of wonder spheres consists of seventy specialized worlds containing thousands upon thousands of replete institutions and organizations devoted to universe training and spirit culture wherein the pilgrims of time are reeducated and reexamined preparatory to their long flight to Havona.*[8]

You approach the superuniverse capital sphere, where beings of such wisdom and authority dwell that their very presence transforms those who approach. Here you are prepared for what lies beyond—the central universe of perfection.

Your purpose has been thoroughly proved; your faith has been tested. By the time you reach Havona, your sincerity has become sublime. Perfection of purpose and divinity of desire, with steadfastness of faith, have secured your entrance to the settled abodes of eternity; your deliverance from the uncertainties of time is full and complete.[9]

Havona awaits—one billion perfect worlds circling the eternal center. These spheres were not evolved. They were created perfect and have always been perfect. Here you encounter beings who never knew imperfection, who find you fascinating precisely because you climbed from below rather than being created above. You traverse seven circuits, each bringing you closer to the center, each revealing deeper dimensions of truth, beauty, and goodness. Wonder does not fade here. It expands.

The pilgrim lands on the receiving planet of Havona, the pilot world of the seventh circuit, with only one endowment of perfection, perfection of purpose. The Universal Father has decreed: 'Be you perfect, even as I am perfect.' That is the astounding invitation-command broadcast to the finite children of the worlds of space.[10]

And finally, Paradise, the motionless Isle at the heart of all things. Here the Universal Father dwells. Here you stand in the presence of infinite deity and are known, completely and lovingly, for who you are and who you have become. Here you are received into the Mortal Corps of Finality, a powerful ensemble of perfected pilgrims who have traversed the entire ascent and now serve throughout the cosmos. Here you understand, at last, what everything was for.

But even Paradise is not the end. The universe continues to evolve. Vast regions of outer space are organizing for purposes not yet revealed. The journey extends into ages beyond imagining, with challenges and adventures that require exactly what you have become—a being who knows both trial and triumph, setback and success, and who carries experiential wisdom no created-perfect being possesses. Your ascent has prepared you for service without end.

Throughout your eternal career, no matter how far you travel, no matter what heights you achieve, you will always have a home. One of the sacred spheres of Paradise will forever be your home address. Even after you achieve Paradise itself, this supernal realm remains the bosom of your eternal origin, the place where the mystery of your fusion is eternally cherished and understood.

And you will not be there alone. When you encounter another ascending mortal on this journey, whether from Earth or elsewhere, you meet a sibling in the most literal sense. The identical nature of the divine fragment indwelling each individual creates a bond that transcends all differences of origin, culture, or biology. All beings in creation ultimately share the same divine Parent. The path is long, but you do not walk it alone.

This is where fusion leads. This is what awaits. The path stretches from wherever you are now, through death, through training worlds, through realms of increasing glory, all the way to the center of reality and beyond. It is real. It is traversable. And everyone who chooses it will arrive.

13

PARADISE

Eventually, after what might be millions of years of service and adventure, you arrive.

Paradise is an actual place—a literal, material reality at the exact center of all things, though its materiality is of a constitution beyond mortal comprehension. It is the most real thing in existence, so real that everything else seems shadowy and insubstantial by comparison.

The material beauty of Paradise consists in the magnificence of its physical perfection; the grandeur of the Isle of God is exhibited in the superb intellectual accomplishments and mind development of its inhabitants; the glory of the central Isle is shown forth in the infinite endowment of divine spirit personality, the light of life.[1]

Here you will witness depths of spiritual beauty and wonders of a most magnificent ensemble--the glory and spiritual splendor of the divine abode.

And Paradise is from eternity; there are neither records nor traditions respecting the origin of this nuclear Isle of Light and Life.[2]

Paradise is not a sphere like planets you've known, but an enormous ellipsoid—essentially flat, with upper, peripheral, and nether surfaces. It does not move or rotate. It is stationary, the fixed gravitational center toward which all energy and matter in the universe are drawn. It is the source and focal point of all universal energy, the ultimate material capital of the Infinite Father.

> *If you had the time and means of passage, were spiritually qualified, and had the necessary guidance, you could be piloted through universe upon universe and from circuit to circuit, ever journeying inward through the starry realms, until at last you would stand before the central shining of the spiritual glory of the Universal Father.*[3]

The gravitational pull of Paradise reaches every world in every universe in all of space. It is the all-powerful grasp of God's physical presence.

> *Gravity is the omnipotent strand on which are strung the gleaming stars, blazing suns, and whirling spheres which constitute the universal physical adornment of the eternal God, who is all things, fills all things, and in whom all things consist.*[4]

On Paradise, you encounter the Trinity. Not three separate gods. Not three aspects of one God. But three persons who are simultaneously distinct and unified—each infinite, each absolute, each fully divine, and yet somehow *one* in ways that transcend finite logic. The Father, the Source of personality, the First Cause. The Son, the eternal Word, the pattern of all spiritual reality. The Spirit, the infinite Actor, the presence you have felt throughout your journey coordinating the systems that made your survival and advancement possible.

There are no words to describe the encounter when you finally stand in the actual presence of the Universal Father himself.

Here is God personally, literally, and actually present. And from his infinite being there flow the flood-streams of life, energy, and personality to all universes.[5]

This is not a temporary dwelling or a symbolic throne. This is the home of God. He has always been here, before time began, before the first universe stirred into existence. Every energy that sustains every world in every universe flows from this place. Every personality ever created traces its origin here.

God dwells, has dwelt, and everlastingly will dwell in this same central and eternal abode. We have always found him there and always will. The Universal Father is cosmically focalized, spiritually personalized, and geographically resident at this center of the universe of universes.[6]

The Father knows you with an intimacy and completeness that no mortal experience can approximate. He knows every thought you ever thought, every choice you ever made, every moment of your existence from your first moral decision as a child to this instant of arrival on Paradise.

And he loves you. Not merely loves humanity in general or spiritual beings in general, but loves *you*, specifically, individually, with a love so personal and so pure that it validates every moment of pain, every moment of doubt, every moment of faith you exercised throughout your entire ascent.

If you will cooperate with your spirit, the divine gift will, sooner or later, evolve the immortal soul and, subsequent to fusion therewith, will present the new creature to the sovereign Master Son of the local universe and eventually to the Father of spirits on Paradise.[7]

This is the complete arc: cooperation leads to soul, soul leads to fusion, fusion leads to the local universe, and the local universe leads to Paradise. The entire journey is contained in that single conditional: if you will cooperate.

But Paradise is not retirement. It is not the end of activity, the beginning of eternal rest. Yes, there is rest—profound, nourishing rest unlike anything you experienced in lower realms.

The one essential to the enjoyment of Paradise is rest, divine rest.[8]

This is not the exhausted collapse of a body that has spent itself. It is the deep, settled stillness of a being that has finally arrived where it belongs. Every tension dissolves. Every striving ceases. Not because there is nothing left to do, but because there is nothing left to prove.

And there is worship—divine exaltation beyond anything you experienced in your long ascent.

While the Isle of Paradise contains certain places of worship, it is more nearly one vast sanctuary of divine service. Worship is the first and dominant passion of all who climb to its blissful shores, the spontaneous ebullition of the beings who have learned enough of God to attain his presence. Circle by circle, during the inward journey through Havona, worship is a growing passion until on Paradise it becomes necessary to direct and otherwise control its expression.

Sometimes all Paradise becomes engulfed in a dominating tide of spiritual and worshipful expression. Often the conductors of worship cannot control such phenomena until the appearance of the threefold fluctuation of the light of the Deity abode, signifying that the divine heart of the Gods has been fully and completely satisfied by the sincere worship of the residents of Paradise, the perfect citizens of glory and the ascendant creatures of time. What a triumph of technique! What a fruition of the eternal plan and purpose of the Gods that the intelligent love of the creature child should give full satisfaction to the infinite love of the Creator Father![9]

And yet, as magnificent as worship becomes on Paradise, it is not the whole of Paradise life. Between these waves of adoration, there is also purpose. There is service, creation, exploration, and deep engagement with other beings from every corner of the cosmos. There is work to be done—divine work.

Work at this level is not draining. It is not obligation grudgingly fulfilled. It is pure joy, the exercise of perfected capacities in perfect environments for perfect purposes. You create from abundance. You contemplate with clarity you could never achieve in lower realms. You form deep friendships with beings from across the cosmos, connections that will endure forever.

Here is the paradox: even on Paradise, even in perfection, you continue to grow. Not from imperfection toward perfection—that journey is complete. But from perfection into greater depths of perfection. There are capacities you develop here that were impossible before. Insights that become accessible only when consciousness reaches Paradise levels. You will never stop exploring, never stop learning, never reach some final state where nothing new is possible.

And standing here, finally arrived at the center of all things, you feel the rise of something within you. The words that echoed across your entire ascent now reach their fulfillment:

The test of time is almost over; the race for eternity has been all but run. The days of uncertainty are ending; the temptation to doubt is vanishing; the injunction to be perfect has been obeyed. From the very bottom of intelligent existence the creature of time and material personality has ascended the evolutionary spheres of space, thus proving the feasibility of the ascension plan while forever demonstrating the justice and righteousness of the command of the Universal Father to his lowly creatures of the worlds: 'Be you perfect, even as I am perfect.'

Step by step, life by life, world by world, the ascendant career has been mastered, and the goal of Deity has been attained. Survival is complete in perfection, and perfection is replete in the supremacy of

You made it. Against all odds—mortal fragility, spiritual immaturity, finite limitation—you made it. From the obscurity of mortal death to the wonders of Paradise glory. From nascent animal consciousness to perfected spiritual awareness.

And you were helped every step of the way. Seraphic guardians protecting you, teachers instructing you, the indwelling spirit guiding you, the Father loving you. You were never alone, never abandoned, never truly lost even in your darkest moments.

And when such an animal-origin being does stand, as countless numbers now do, before the Gods on Paradise, having ascended from the lowly spheres of space, such an achievement represents the reality of a spiritual transformation bordering on the limits of supremacy.[11]

And what a being you have become through this age-long metamorphosis!

They are indeed the accumulating tried and true souls of time and space, the evolutionary salt of the universe, and they are forever proof against evil and secure against sin.[12]

Death was not the end. It was the beginning. You made it. You are home. Finally, fully, forever home.

Paradise is glorious. And perfect. You have become, through your long ascent, a being who understands both imperfection and perfection. You have experienced failure and victory, ignorance and wisdom, doubt and faith. Your long career of universe training prepared you for more than Paradise. So you join the Corps of the Finality.

While the finaliters serve in various capacities, they are also held in reserve for a purpose not yet fully revealed. But the sense is clear: something vast is coming. Some future age, some cosmic project, some challenge or adventure on a scale that dwarfs even the grand universe.

> *There actually is a vast and new system of universes gradually organizing in the domains of outer space. New orders of physical creations, enormous and gigantic circles of swarming universes upon universes far out beyond the present bounds of the peopled and organized creations, are actually visible through your telescopes.*[13]

And the finaliters, beings who combine humanity and divinity, who understand both the lowest and highest reaches of reality, will be essential to it.

Even as finaliters you remain what the universe calls sixth-stage spirits. There are heights beyond even this. The journey from mortal origin to Paradise perfection, vast as it is, represents only the beginning of an even greater adventure.

> *The mortal finaliters have fully complied with the injunction of the ages, 'Be you perfect'; they have ascended the universal path of mortal attainment; they have found God, and they have been duly inducted into the Corps of the Finality. Such beings have attained the present limit of spirit progression but not finality of ultimate spirit status. They have achieved the present limit of creature perfection but not finality of creature service. They have experienced the fullness of Deity worship but not finality of experiential Deity attainment.*[14]

What awaits beyond the current universe age? An undisclosed and universal adventure in the experience of exploring the infinity of the Universal Father. You will be starting out on the quest for the superfinite Father—seeking to know dimensions of deity that transcend even what you have experienced in Paradise. Eternity is not repetition; it is endless discovery.

Now have these two identities become one; no event of time or of eter-nity can ever separate man and the divine spirit; they are inseparable, eternally fused.[15]

You discover that fusion gave you more than immortality. It gave you a *destiny*—a role to play in the cosmic drama, a contribution to make to the universal project of bringing everything to perfection. You are not just a survivor. You are not just a successful graduate of the ascension school. You are a *cosmic resource*, a being of unique value, prepared for purposes even Paradise administrators can only dimly glimpse.

What an adventure! What a romance! A gigantic creation to be administered by the children of the Supreme, these personalized and humanized Adjusters, these spiritized and eternalized mortals, these mysterious combinations and eternal associations of the highest known manifestation of the essence of the First Source and Center and the lowest form of intelligent life capable of comprehending and attaining the Universal Father.[16]

And you realize: this is what you were made for. Not just to survive, not just to be happy, but to have your existence make a difference on the largest possible scale.

Evolutionary mortals are born on the planets of space, pass through the morontia worlds, ascend the spirit universes, traverse the Havona spheres, find God, attain Paradise, and are mustered into the primary Corps of the Finality, therein to await the next assignment of universe service. And as we view this sublime spectacle, we all exclaim: What a glorious destiny for the animal-origin children of time, the material sons of space![17]

14

THE FAMILY

One of the most beautiful aspects of fusion and eternal life is that your relationships don't end. They continue, they deepen, they become more profound and more meaningful than any human relationship possibly could be.

Your family members who passed on, you will see them again. You will recognize them. You will love them with a love purified of all the petty annoyances and misunderstandings that clouded mortal relationships.

> *Love is the desire to do good to others. Love is the ancestor of all spiritual goodness, the essence of the true and the beautiful.*[1]

The connection you felt to your parents, your children, your spouse, your dearest friends—these connections are eternal, and they grow richer with time.

A natural question arises: Will I really know them? After death, after all the changes that come with the transition to a new form of existence, will my mother still be my mother? Will my friend still be my friend?

The answer is yes. Personality persists. The essential person you loved continues, and you will recognize them immediately.

> *Personality is that part of any individual which enables us to recognize and positively identify that person as the one we have previously known, no matter how much he may have changed because of the modification of the vehicle of expression and manifestation of his personality.*[2]

The body changes. The mind expands. But the person, the unique configuration of character and identity that made them who they were, that remains. And your capacity to recognize those you love remains as well.

Upon awakening on the mansion worlds, you have ten days of personal liberty to explore your new surroundings and reconnect with those who preceded you.

> *You are free to explore the immediate vicinity of your new home and to familiarize yourself with the program which lies immediately ahead. You also have time to gratify your desire to consult the registry and call upon your loved ones and other earth friends who may have preceded you to these worlds.*[3]

This recognition is not merely intellectual. It is personal and emotional. The bonds forged in mortal life are not erased—they are purified and strengthened. What was temporary becomes permanent. What was partial becomes complete.

Why does family matter so much? Because it is where you first learn the lessons that matter most in eternity.

In family life, you learn to love people you didn't choose. You learn patience with those who frustrate you. You learn sacrifice—putting another's needs before your own. You learn forgiveness, because living closely with anyone eventually requires it.

Almost everything of lasting value in civilization has its roots in the family. The family was the first successful peace group, the man and woman learning how to adjust their antagonisms while at the same time teaching the pursuits of peace to their children.[4]

The family is not merely a social institution. It is a spiritual training ground. The skills you develop there—how to love, how to serve, how to cooperate, how to resolve conflict—these are the very skills you will need throughout your eternal career.

When a wise man understands the inner impulses of his fellows, he will love them. And when you love your brother, you have already forgiven him. This capacity to understand man's nature and forgive his apparent wrongdoing is Godlike.[5]

The forgiveness you learn in family life, the understanding you develop for those closest to you—this prepares you for the universal family you are about to join.

If you are a parent, you have been given a profound spiritual education. You know what it means to love someone more than yourself. You know the ache of watching your child struggle and being unable to fix it for them. You know the joy of seeing them succeed.

The experience of loving as a parent loves teaches you something about God that no theology can convey. When you hold your child for the first time and feel that surge of protective, unconditional love, you glimpse how God feels about you. A good parent loves unconditionally, provides generously, guides patiently, and rejoices in the child's growth. This is precisely how God relates to you.

Marriage, with children and consequent family life, is stimulative of the highest potentials in human nature and simultaneously provides the ideal avenue for the expression of these quickened attributes of mortal personality.[6]

Since we were all children at one point, we have learned what it means to trust, to be provided for, to be guided by someone wiser. These experiences prepare us to relate rightly to our heavenly Parent.

The quality of your early family life shapes your capacity to understand God. This is why healthy families are so important. If your early family was not healthy, take heart: the indwelling spirit works to heal those wounds and to give you a truer picture of divine parenthood than your earthly parents could provide. And the family you are joining extends far beyond the one you were born into.

But you also form new relationships, friendships with beings from other worlds, from other species, from other cultures so different from human that you can barely imagine them now. You discover that love and friendship and connection are universal realities, present wherever personal beings exist.

No man is a stranger to one who knows God. In the experience of finding the Father in heaven you discover that all men are your brothers, and does it seem strange that one should enjoy the exhilaration of meeting a newly discovered brother? To become acquainted with one's brothers and sisters, to know their problems and to learn to love them, is the supreme experience of living.[7]

But even as your family expands across the cosmos, you remain connected to Earth. You don't forget where you came from. Many fused beings volunteer to return to the evolutionary worlds in various capacities—as unseen guides, as helpers working behind the scenes to foster spiritual evolution.

You can serve humanity from a position of knowledge and power and authority. And many do, because love compels them, because they remember what it was like to toil in darkness, because they desire for others what they themselves have achieved.

One of the most beautiful revelations that comes with understanding fusion is this: you are not just an individual destined for personal immortality. You are part of a vast family of ascending beings, all making the same journey, all climbing toward the same destination.

> *You become conscious of man as your creature brother because you are already conscious of God as your Creator Father. Fatherhood is the relationship out of which we reason ourselves into the recognition of brotherhood. And Fatherhood becomes, or may become, a universe reality to all moral creatures because the Father has himself bestowed personality upon all such beings and has encircuited them within the grasp of the universal personality circuit.*[8]

Right now, across millions of inhabited worlds, other mortals are reading or hearing words similar to these. They are learning about their indwelling spirits. They are discovering their destiny. They are cooperating consciously with the process of an eternal unfolding.

Someday, somewhere in eternity, you will meet them. You will compare experiences. You will share stories of your respective worlds. You will find common ground across gulfs that seem unbridgeable now—different species, different biology, different evolutionary histories—because underneath it all, you share the fundamental experience of being finite creatures climbing toward infinite perfection.

> *They are ever drawn towards his Paradise presence by that kinship of being which constitutes the vast and universal family circle and fraternal circuit of the eternal God.*[9]

This is what draws you. This is what draws them. Across every world and every species, the same gravity of kinship pulls all persons toward the same center.

This family extends beyond ascending mortals. It includes not only your guardian seraphim but other angels serving in countless capacities throughout the universes.

Your guardian angel knows you intimately. She has watched over you since childhood. She has worked to arrange circumstances for your spiritual benefit. She has rejoiced at your victories and grieved at your failures. She is, in a very real sense, family.

> *The guardian seraphim is the custodial trustee of the survival values of mortal man's slumbering soul as the indwelling spirit is the identity of such an immortal universe being. When these two collaborate in the resurrection halls of mansonia in conjunction with the newly fabricated morontia form, there occurs the reassembly of the constituent factors of the personality of the mortal ascender.*[10]

After your death, she guards your soul during the transition. When you awaken on the mansion worlds, she is there—one of the first beings you meet, someone who knows your entire history, someone who has loved you through it all.

This family also includes administrators and teachers and creators of various orders. It includes beings who were never mortal, who began their existence at higher levels of reality.

All of these beings are your family. All of them recognize you, after fusion, as a full member of the cosmic community. All of them celebrate your achievement, because your success enriches the entire universe.

This understanding of universal family is not meant to remain abstract. It should change how you live now—how you treat strangers, how you regard those different from yourself, how you respond to those in need.

If all humans are your siblings, if every person you meet carries the same divine indwelling, if everyone is destined for the same eternal adventure, then how can you hate? How can you dismiss? How can you pass by someone in need without being moved?

The family of God is not merely a future reality. It exists now. You are already part of it. The question is whether you will live as though you are.

And at the head of this family stands the Universal Father—a perfect and loving parent, delighted by your achievements, invested in your success, absolutely present in your life through the divine gift.

You are loved. You belong. You are part of a reality infinitely larger than yourself, yet you matter individually within it. This realization of universal kinship leads somewhere. It fosters lasting joy, unselfish service, genuine care for strangers, and cooperation across every boundary.

15

ETERNITY IN VIEW

WHEN YOU TRULY GRASP THAT YOU ARE DESTINED FOR ETERNITY, THERE can be substantial changes in how you view your current life.

The things that consume most people's attention—accumulating wealth, achieving status, winning arguments, nursing grudges—suddenly seem trivial. They take their proper size in relation to eternity.

You're going to live forever. Trillions of years from now, you will still exist, still growing, still serving, still experiencing new realities. It is the direct consequence of what God has done—his giving of himself to his creatures creates a boundless, almost inconceivable future possibility of progressive and successive existences for these divinely endowed mortals.

From that perspective, whether you own a large house or a small one, whether you achieve fame or remain obscure, whether people praise you or criticize you—these things matter far less than how they shape your character.

Did that wealth make you more generous or more fearful? Did that fame make you more humble or more arrogant? Did that criticism make you more reflective or more defensive? That's what matters, because that's what you take with you. Everything else stays behind.

> *Time is the one universal endowment of all will creatures. It is the talent entrusted to all intelligent beings. You all have time in which to ensure your survival.[1]*

This perspective is enormously liberating. It frees you from the tyranny of the urgent. It allows you to make choices based on eternal values rather than immediate pressures. It gives you patience, the ability to endure temporary difficulties knowing they will end, while what you become lasts forever.

But to be clear: this eternal perspective doesn't make you immune to suffering. It might even increase certain kinds of suffering, because you become more sensitive to how things are and how they ought to be.

> *Religious perplexities are inevitable; there can be no progress without psychic conflict and spiritual agitation.[2]*

You will still experience loss. Loved ones will die, relationships will end, dreams will fail. You will still face injustice, illness, disappointment, and pain. The world will still be broken in countless ways, and your spiritual development won't fix it immediately.

But what changes is how you experience these difficulties.

You experience them with hope, because you know they're temporary. This life's sorrows are real but limited. They cannot follow you beyond death.

You experience them with meaning, because you understand that difficulty develops character in ways ease never could. The patience, compassion, faith, and strength you develop through suffering are eternal gains.

The measure of the spiritual capacity of the evolving soul is your faith in truth and your love for man, but the measure of your human strength of character is your ability to resist the holding of grudges and your capacity to withstand brooding in the face of deep sorrow. Defeat is the true mirror in which you may honestly view your real self.[3]

You experience them with peace, because underneath all the turbulence is the unchanging reality of God's love and your eternal security. The storms rage on the surface, but in the depths there is stillness.

When the flood tides of human adversity, selfishness, cruelty, hate, malice, and jealousy beat about the mortal soul, you may rest in the assurance that there is one inner bastion, the citadel of the spirit, which is absolutely unassailable; at least this is true of every human being who has dedicated the keeping of his soul to the indwelling spirit of the eternal God.[4]

And from this unassailable place comes a peace unlike anything the world offers—a dynamic and sublime peace that passes all human understanding, a cosmic poise that is immune to disappointment.

Such spirit-born individuals are so remotivated in life that they can calmly stand by while their fondest ambitions perish and their keenest hopes crash; they positively know that such catastrophes are but the redirecting cataclysms that wreck one's temporal creations preparatory to the rearing of more noble and enduring realities.[5]

You experience these difficulties with joy—deep, unshakeable joy that comes from knowing your life has purpose, your hardships have meaning, and your destiny is secure.

The highest happiness is indissolubly linked with spiritual progress. Spiritual growth yields lasting joy, peace which passes all understanding.[6]

This paradox is real: you can be simultaneously sad and joyful, grieving and hopeful, suffering and at peace. The mortal mind may want to resolve it into simple either-or. But spiritual maturity embraces the complexity, holds both realities at once.

You weep with those who weep. You feel their pain. But underneath it all, you know that this is not the end, that beauty will triumph, that love wins, that every tear will be wiped away and every wrong made right.

And yet this eternal perspective doesn't pull you out of the present. It intensifies it. You are no longer looking at the universe from the outside, as a lonely creature wondering if any of it means anything. You are looking at it from within.

> *Such faith-liberated sons have certainly enlisted in the struggles of time on the side of the supreme forces and divine personalities of eternity; even the stars in their courses are now doing battle for them; at last they gaze upon the universe from within, from God's viewpoint, and all is transformed from the uncertainties of material isolation to the sureties of eternal spiritual progression. Even time itself becomes but the shadow of eternity cast by Paradise realities upon the moving panoply of space.*[7]

When you know that your choices carry significant weight, you take them more seriously. When you know that relationships can continue eternally, you invest in them more deeply. When you know that character is the only thing you get to keep, you pay attention to its development.

And the place where character develops is here. Now. This moment.

Spiritual transformation is not a single event but a process, built choice by choice, day by day. What you consistently choose is what you consistently become.

> *Virtue is righteousness—conformity with the cosmos. To name virtues is not to define them, but to live them is to know them. Virtue is not*

Most people live half-asleep, moving through their days on autopilot, lost in thoughts about past or future, barely noticing what's actually happening right now. This unconscious living is the enemy of spiritual development, because the indwelling spirit works in the present moment. It can only influence the thoughts you're actually thinking, the choices you're actually making, the reality you're actually experiencing.

To cooperate with your spirit is to become more present, more aware, more conscious, more fully engaged with each moment. It means noticing your thoughts without being controlled by them, observing when you're being judgmental or anxious or defensive, and choosing to redirect toward truth, peace, and patience. It means listening when people speak, instead of waiting for your turn to talk. Every person you encounter carries their own spirit of divinity. Treat them accordingly.

Presence means experiencing beauty fully when you encounter it—in nature, in art, in human kindness. Beauty is a revelation of divine reality. Don't rush past it. Presence means choosing consciously instead of reacting automatically. That moment between stimulus and response—that's where spiritual transformation happens. Expand that moment. Use it.

This practice doesn't require special circumstances or dedicated time, though those help. It can happen anywhere—while washing dishes, sitting in traffic, talking with a friend, or working at your job. Every moment is an opportunity for conscious cooperation with God.

Mind is your ship, the indwelling spirit is your pilot, the human will is captain. The master of the mortal vessel should have the wisdom to trust the divine pilot to guide the ascending soul into the harbors of eternal survival.[9]

Some of the most powerful moments of contact with your spirit come not in quiet meditation but in active service—when you forget yourself entirely in caring for another, when your ego steps aside and love flows unimpeded. These moments of self-forgetting are windows through which the Divine can work most powerfully.

The imitation of God is the key to perfection; the doing of his will is the secret of survival and of perfection in survival.[10]

Presence ultimately becomes imitation. Not merely noticing God, but becoming like God—in how you love, how you serve, how you engage with each moment and each person. Living with eternity in view means living fully now. And the person who lives this way—who has tasted the reality of God, who has felt the spirit's presence, who has dedicated their will to the Father's purposes—carries something that nothing in this world can take away.

The convictions of such an experience are unassailable; the logic of religious living is incontrovertible; the certainty of such knowledge is superhuman; the satisfactions are superbly divine, the courage indomitable, the devotions unquestioning, the loyalties supreme, and the destinies final—eternal, ultimate, and universal.[11]

EPILOGUE

HERE, THEN, IS THE TRUTH THAT MOST PEOPLE LIVE AND DIE WITHOUT realizing:

Within you, right now, dwells a fragment of God. It will remain there until fusion occurs or until you definitively reject it. It loves you with perfect love. It is working constantly toward your eternal survival and eventual perfection.

This is the literal truth of your existence. And this indwelling presence is inviting you—has been inviting you every day of your life—into conscious partnership, into deliberate cooperation, into full awareness of what is happening and willing participation in it.

> *The indwelling spirit is the essence of man's perfected personality, which he can foretaste in time as he progressively masters the divine technique of achieving the living of the Father's will.*[1]

You don't have to be perfect to respond to this invitation. You don't have to have your theology figured out. You don't have to be smarter or holier or better than you are. You just have to be willing.

Willing to believe that spiritual realities are real. Willing to try living as if your life has eternal significance. Willing to love sincerely, serve humbly, seek truth honestly. Willing to worship, to experience the supreme satisfaction of communion with God. Willing to trust that the universe is friendly, that you are held, that you are wanted, that you are going somewhere worth going.

> *The doing of the will of God is nothing more or less than an exhibition of creature willingness to share the inner life with God—with the very God who has made such a creature life of inner meaning-value possible.*[2]

If you can move in this direction, even imperfectly, the spirit will work with what you give it. Your soul will grow. Your character will develop. And eventually, whether in this life or the next, you will reach the doors to divine fusion.

And when it happens, when that moment of eternal unity finally arrives, you will understand—fully, completely, joyously—that *this* was what everything was leading toward. All the effort, all the growth, all the difficult choices and painful lessons—they were preparing you for this.

For union with God. For eternity. For a destiny more magnificent than any human mind can imagine.

> *When mortal man fuses with an actual fragment of the existential Cause of the total cosmos, no limit can ever be placed upon the destiny of such an unprecedented and unimaginable partnership.*[3]

The invitation stands. It has always stood. It will continue to stand for as long as you live.

How will you respond?

COMMON QUESTIONS

By now you may have questions, doubts or concerns that what you've read sounds too good to be true, or too strange to accept, or too demanding to attempt.

Such questions are natural. The truths presented here challenge assumptions most people have carried their entire lives. They raise questions that deserve honest answers.

What if I've made terrible choices? What if I've wasted years being selfish or cruel or faithless?

Start now. The past is past. The Father's gift doesn't abandon you because you've made mistakes. It has infinite patience. It will work with you from wherever you are, no matter how far you've strayed, no matter how much you've failed. The moment you turn toward the Father, the entire universe mobilizes to help you.

What if I'm not religious? What if I don't believe in God in traditional ways?

That's fine. The divine spirit doesn't require orthodox theology. It requires sincerity, genuine desire for truth, and willingness to grow.

Some of the most spiritually advanced people have been those who rejected religion but lived lives of extraordinary integrity, love, and service. Doctrine matters far less than character.

> *If any man chooses to do the divine will, he shall know the way of truth. The assurance that the spirit dwells within is experiential, not merely intellectual.*[1]

What if I'm afraid of eternity? What if the idea of living forever terrifies me?

That fear is natural from a mortal perspective. But eternity is thrilling. You won't be bored. Infinite reality stretches before you—endless worlds to discover, limitless truths to learn, ever new ways to serve and create and love. The fear comes from imagining eternity with your current limited consciousness. But you won't have that consciousness. You will have one far greater. And eternity is nothing like life on Earth.

What if I fail? What if I don't make it to fusion?

Failure is possible but uncommon. The Father wants you to succeed. The divine gift is working tirelessly toward your survival. Angels are assisting you. The entire universe is on your side.

> *At last all creatures become conscious of the fact that God and all the divine hosts of a well-nigh limitless universe are on their side in the supernal struggle to attain eternity of life and divinity of status. Such faith-liberated sons have certainly enlisted in the struggles of time on the side of the supreme forces and divine personalities of eternity; even the stars in their courses are now doing battle for them.*[2]

You would have to willfully, persistently reject all help to fail. And even then, even at the last moment, if you change your mind, the door remains open.

How do I know any of this is real? How do I know I'm not just imagining the indwelling spirit?

You can't prove inner experience to anyone else. You can't put the spirit under a microscope or measure communion with instruments.

Your spiritual intuitions might be projections. Or they might be perceptions—the forecasts of a spirit that dwells within you, showing you realities your material eyes cannot see. The only way to know is to test them.

Try the technique. Practice communion. See what happens to your character, your peace, your capacity to love. If nothing changes, perhaps it was imagination. But if you find yourself becoming more patient, more loving, more at peace, more aligned with truth—something real is at work.

Isn't this just wishful thinking? Humans want eternal life and cosmic significance, so they invent stories that provide it.

Maybe. But consider the contradiction at the heart of that claim: the assertion 'we are only matter' is made by something that matter cannot produce. Machines don't doubt. Atoms don't wonder. Molecules don't hunger for meaning. The very act of questioning whether spiritual realities are real requires a consciousness that pure materialism cannot explain.

And notice what you hunger for: truth, beauty, goodness, meaning, love. These aren't chemical reactions. Physics doesn't care about justice. Chemistry has no opinion on beauty. Yet you recognize these things instantly, and their absence disturbs you. Why? If you were only a machine, you would be wholly unconscious of the fact. The pessimist who despairs that life has no meaning has already demonstrated that he is more than matter—because matter cannot despair.

What about people who never heard of any of this? What about people who died without knowing?

They wake up in the next life. And there they are taught everything we're discussing here. No one is disadvantaged by dying in ignorance. The opportunity for fusion is universal, available to every normal-minded person regardless of when or where they lived or what they knew or didn't know.

Does fusion mean I lose my individuality? Do I become absorbed into God?

No. Absolutely not. Your personality, your unique identity, is eternal and inviolable. Fusion enhances it, stabilizes it, and perfects it. You become more yourself, not less. You don't disappear into God. You become united with God while remaining distinctly you.

FROM THE AUTHOR

Thank you for reading. This book is the culmination of twenty years of spiritual seeking, study, and reflection.

If you're willing to share your thoughts, reader reviews make a meaningful difference for independent authors. Thank you so much.

APPENDIX

The information in this book is drawn from *The Urantia Book*, a 2,097 page book first published in 1955 that claims to be a revelation presented by celestial beings to clarify and expand human understanding of cosmic reality and our place within it. This book about angels exclusively cites the 1955 edition which is in the public domain.

You may have never heard of it. Or you may have heard of it and dismissed it. That's fine. What matters is whether the information resonates as true, whether it elevates your understanding, whether it helps you live with greater purpose and confidence.

The Urantia Book has its critics and its devoted students. It's been called everything from the most important spiritual text of the modern era to elaborate fiction. I'm not asking you to accept it blindly. I'm asking you to read it and *then* decide if you think it is true. I do, and I have read it countless times.

The source is less important than the truth it contains. And if you want to explore further, *The Urantia Book* is available online and in print.

About The Source Material

The Urantia Book is a comprehensive revelatory tome covering a wide variety of subjects including cosmology, philosophy, history and spirituality. It describes the nature of reality from the perspective of celestial beings and provides detailed information about the structure of the universe, the nature of God, the purpose of human existence, and the journey of the soul after death.

The book is organized into 196 papers grouped into four parts:

Part I: The Central and Superuniverses

Part II: The Local Universe

Part III: The History of Urantia (Earth)

Part IV: The Life and Teachings of Jesus

While I do, at times, exercise creative license, my intention is never to stray from what the book discloses as revelatory fact. Any mistakes are mine to own and correct.

Italicized passages throughout this book are drawn from The Urantia Book, either verbatim or closely paraphrased. Many have been slightly condensed, combined, edited, or adapted for brevity and narrative continuity while preserving the essential meaning and terminology of the original text.

The following references are organized by chapter to help readers locate the source material corresponding to specific content in this book.

NOTES

INTRODUCTION

1. Paper 107, Introduction: Origin and Nature of Thought Adjusters
2. Paper 107, Introduction: Origin and Nature of Thought Adjusters
3. Paper 11, Section 9: The Eternal Isle of Paradise, The Uniqueness of Paradise

1. THE GIFT

1. Paper 1, Section 4: The Universal Father, The Mystery of God
2. Paper 110, Section 0: Relation of Adjusters to Individual Mortals, Introduction
3. Paper 107, Section 0: Origin and Nature of Thought Adjusters, Introduction
4. Paper 5, Section 2: God's Relation to the Individual, The Presence of God
5. Paper 5, Section 1: God's Relation to the Individual, The Approach to God
6. Paper 5, Section 6: God's Relation to the Individual, The God of Personality
7. Paper 107, Section 0: Origin and Nature of Thought Adjusters, Introduction
8. Paper 107, Section 0: Origin and Nature of Thought Adjusters, Introduction
9. Paper 107, Section 1: Origin and Nature of Thought Adjusters, Origin of Thought Adjusters
10. Paper 108, Section 0: Mission and Ministry of Thought Adjusters, Introduction
11. Paper 110, Section 0: Relation of Adjusters to Individual Mortals, Introduction
12. Paper 101, Section 1: The Real Nature of Religion, True Religion
13. Paper 101, Section 1: The Real Nature of Religion, True Religion
14. Paper 109, Section 6: Relation of Adjusters to Universe Creatures, The Persistence of True Values
15. Paper 103, Section 0: The Reality of Religious Experience, Introduction

2. THE GIVER

1. Paper 1, Section 5: The Universal Father, Personality of the Universal Father
2. Paper 1, Section 0: The Universal Father, Introduction
3. Paper 4, Section 4: God's Relation to the Universe, The Realization of God
4. Paper 2, Section 4: The Nature of God, The Divine Mercy
5. Paper 2, Section 5: The Nature of God, The Love of God
6. Paper 4, Section 3: God's Relation to the Universe, God's Unchanging Character
7. Paper 2, Section 5: The Nature of God, The Love of God
8. Paper 5, Section 0: God's Relation to the Individual, Introduction
9. Paper 2, Section 1: The Nature of God, The Infinity of God
10. Paper 1, Section 7: The Universal Father, Spiritual Value of the Personality Concept
11. Paper 2, Section 5: The Nature of God, The Love of God

3. THE PARTNERSHIP

4. THE SOUL

5. FUSION

6. Paper 112, Section 7: Personality Survival, Adjuster Fusion
7. Paper 107, Section 0: Origin and Nature of Thought Adjusters, Introduction

6. THE SEVEN CIRCLES

1. Paper 110, Section 6: Relation of Adjusters to Individual Mortals, The Seven Psychic Circles
2. Paper 110, Section 6: Relation of Adjusters to Individual Mortals, The Seven Psychic Circles
3. Paper 110, Section 7: Relation of Adjusters to Individual Mortals, The Attainment of Immortality
4. Paper 110, Section 6: Relation of Adjusters to Individual Mortals, The Seven Psychic Circles
5. Paper 110, Section 7: Relation of Adjusters to Individual Mortals, The Attainment of Immortality
6. Paper 110, Section 3: Relation of Adjusters to Individual Mortals, Cooperation with the Adjuster
7. Paper 110, Section 6: Relation of Adjusters to Individual Mortals, The Seven Psychic Circles

7. THE TRANSFORMATION

1. Paper 107, Section 0: Origin and Nature of Thought Adjusters, Introduction
2. Paper 109, Section 3: Relation of Adjusters to Universe Creatures, Relation of Adjusters to Mortal Types
3. Paper 112, Section 7: Personality Survival, Adjuster Fusion
4. Paper 100, Section 6: Religion in Human Experience, Marks of Religious Living
5. Paper 112, Section 7: Personality Survival, Adjuster Fusion
6. Paper 112, Section 7: Personality Survival, Adjuster Fusion

8. COOPERATION

1. Paper 108, Section 5: Mission and Ministry of Thought Adjusters, The Adjuster's Mission
2. Paper 100, Section 1: Religion in Human Experience, Religious Growth
3. Paper 100, Section 2: Religion in Human Experience, Spiritual Growth
4. Paper 110, Section 3: Relation of Adjusters to Individual Mortals, Cooperation with the Adjuster
5. Paper 102, Section 6: The Foundations of Religious Faith, The Certainty of Religious Faith
6. Paper 111, Section 5: The Adjuster and the Soul, The Consecration of Choice
7. Paper 100, Section 4: Religion in Human Experience, Problems of Growth
8. Paper 91, Section 7: The Evolution of Prayer, Mysticism, Ecstasy, and Inspiration
9. Paper 100, Section 2: Religion in Human Experience, Spiritual Growth
10. Paper 110, Section 3: Relation of Adjusters to Individual Mortals, Cooperation with the Adjuster

9. COMMUNION

1. Paper 102, Section 1: The Foundations of Religious Faith, Assurances of Faith
2. Paper 3, Section 1: The Attributes of God, God's Everywhereness
3. Paper 110, Section 7: Relation of Adjusters to Individual Mortals, The Attainment of Immortality
4. Andrew Newberg et al., "Cerebral blood flow during meditative prayer: preliminary findings and methodological issues," Perceptual and Motor Skills 97, no. 2 (2003): 625-30. This preliminary study of three Franciscan nuns practicing centering prayer showed increased blood flow in the prefrontal cortex (7.1%), inferior parietal lobes (6.8%), and inferior frontal lobes (9.0%).
5. Brewer et al., "Meditation experience is associated with differences in default mode network activity and connectivity," Proceedings of the National Academy of Sciences 108, no. 50 (2011): 20254-59. Experienced meditators showed stronger coupling between brain regions implicated in self-monitoring and cognitive control, both at baseline and during meditation.
6. Newberg and Waldman discuss how contemplative practices affect brain function, reduce stress hormones, and promote emotional regulation. See How God Changes Your Brain: Breakthrough Findings from a Leading Neuroscientist (Ballantine Books, 2009).
7. Individuals who participated in an eight-week mindfulness program showed increased gray matter concentration in the left hippocampus. Hölzel et al., "Mindfulness practice leads to increases in regional brain gray matter density," Psychiatry Research: Neuroimaging 191, no. 1 (2011): 36–43. In a related study, reductions in perceived stress correlated with decreased gray matter density in the right amygdala. Hölzel et al., "Stress reduction correlates with structural changes in the amygdala," Social Cognitive and Affective Neuroscience 5, no. 1 (2010): 11–17.
8. Newberg and Waldman document that prayer and spiritual practice reduce stress and anxiety and can support immune function. See How God Changes Your Brain (Ballantine Books, 2009).
9. Paper 5, Section 3: God's Relation to the Individual, True Worship
10. Paper 143, Section 7: Going Through Samaria, Teachings About Prayer and Worship
11. Paper 144, Section 4: At Gilboa and in the Decapolis, Prayer and Worship
12. Paper 144, Section 4: At Gilboa and in the Decapolis, Prayer and Worship
13. Paper 91, Section 4: The Evolution of Prayer, Ethical Praying
14. Paper 91, Section 9: The Evolution of Prayer, Conditions of Effective Prayer
15. Paper 144, Section 4: At Gilboa and in the Decapolis, More About Prayer
16. Paper 143, Section 7: Going Through Samaria, Teachings About Prayer and Worship
17. Paper 143, Section 7: Going Through Samaria, Teachings About Prayer and Worship
18. Paper 39, Section 4: The Seraphic Hosts, Administrator Seraphim
19. Paper 110, Section 3: Relation of Adjusters to Individual Mortals, Cooperation with the Adjuster
20. Paper 110, Section 3: Relation of Adjusters to Individual Mortals, Cooperation with the Adjuster

14. THE FAMILY

15. ETERNITY IN VIEW

EPILOGUE

1. Paper 107, Section 0: Origin and Nature of Thought Adjusters, Introduction
2. Paper 111, Section 5: The Adjuster and the Soul, The Consecration of Choice
3. Paper 107, Section 0: Origin and Nature of Thought Adjusters, Introduction

COMMON QUESTIONS

1. Paper 102, Section 1: The Foundations of Religious Faith, Assurances of Faith
2. Paper 101, Section 10: The Real Nature of Religion, Religion as Man's Liberator

ABOUT THE AUTHOR

Michael Vincent spent years searching for answers that religion couldn't provide. Then he discovered *The Urantia Book*—a dense revelation that answered his questions with a coherence he'd never encountered.

His work translates this complex material into books anyone can absorb. Not spiritual platitudes—specific, detailed information about how reality actually works.

Fusion with God is part of that project. Other books cover angels, cosmic history, Jesus, human origins, and the structure of the universe itself.

michaelvincentauthor.com

instagram.com/michaelvincent_author
tiktok.com/@michael.vincent.author
amazon.com/author/havona-press
youtube.com/@MichaelVincent-Author
facebook.com/HavonaPress

ALSO BY MICHAEL VINCENT

The Missing Years: The Real Story of Jesus Beyond the Gospels (The *Universe Maker from Nazareth* series, Book One)

Where We Go When We Die: Life After Death Across the Universe

The Angelic Orders: Cosmic Servants of the Infinite

Upcoming Books:

The Public Ministry: The Real Story of Jesus Beyond the Gospels (The *Universe Maker from Nazareth* series, Book Two)

The Final Week: The Real Story of Jesus Beyond the Gospels (The *Universe Maker from Nazareth* series, Book Three)

The Nine Races: The Forgotten Origin of Humanity

Before Humans: The Drama of World-Making

Marcus Aurelius, Rodan of Alexandria, and Jesus of Nazareth: A Philosopher's Journey